SOMETHING IN THE BLOOD

BY GARY ORCHARD

For more information about this book or others, visit
www.emp3books.com

Published in September 2024 by emp3books Ltd
6 Silvester Way, Church Crookham, Fleet, GU52 0TD

©Gary Orchard 2024

ISBN: 9781910734582

The author asserts the moral right to be identified as the author of this work. All views are those of the author.

All rights reserved. No part of this publication may be reproduced, stored in a retrieval system, or transmitted, in any form or by any means, electronic, mechanical, photocopying, recording or otherwise without the prior written consent of the author.

Limit of Liability/ Disclaimer of Warranty. Whilst the author and publisher have used their best efforts in preparing this book, they make no representation or warranties with respect to the accuracy or completeness of this book and specifically disclaim any warranties of completeness or saleability or fitness of purpose. Neither the author nor the publisher shall be liable for any damages, including but not limited to special, incidental, consequential or any other damages.

Historical characters appear in this publication. All other characters are fictitious and any resemblance to real persons, living or dead, is purely coincidental.

CONTENTS

LONDON 1888	**1**
PRESENT DAY	**7**
1	7
2	11
3	13
4	18
5	20
6	22
7	30
8	36
9	39
10	42
11	47
12	52
13	54
14	60
15	67
16	68
17	70
18	74
19	79
20	82
21	86
22	92
23	98
24	100
25	101
LONDON 1888	**112**
PRESENT DAY	**190**
26	190
27	193
28	195
29	199

30	203
31	207
32	209
33	210
34	211
35	216
36	217
37	221
38	224
39	225
40	227
41	229
42	230
43	233
44	234
45	238
Author's Note	**241**
DEDICATION	**241**

LONDON 1888

'COLVERSON!'

Sergeant Thicke screamed the name in order to make himself heard over the Tower of Babel that Whitechapel police station had been transformed into by the latest edition of the Pall Mall Gazette. The latest atrocity committed by the individual christened by that self-same publication "Jack the Ripper" had made headline news. The Gazette's editor, W. T. Stead, had written a blistering editorial eviscerating the police for their inability to apprehend the Whitechapel fiend, ending with the offer of a hundred guinea reward payable to anyone able to provide the police with information leading to his capture. It was this pecuniary incentive that led to the siege of Peel Street by individuals keen to set the full force of the law on friends, relatives and even complete strangers who had committed some transgression against them, none of which, in Sergeant Thicke's opinion, had anything to do with the Ripper murders and everything to do with the chance to make easy money. In the past five minutes alone, Sergeant Thicke had dealt with a woman who claimed her husband must be the Ripper because he frequented houses of ill repute and beat her bloody when in his cups, something which Sergeant Thicke regarded as a normal state of married affairs and a man whose neighbour regularly came home covered in blood, who, on cursory questioning, turned out to be a butcher!

Sergeant Thicke raised the volume of his already

considerable vocal tones and shouted: 'You'll not get paid, not one penny piece, unless we make an arrest, you know that don't you? It doesn't matter what blasted W. T. Stead says in his sainted Gazette. Not one penny piece, do you hear me?'

Whether they heard or not, it made not one whit of difference to the clamouring throng who sought to press their claim for whatever financial reward may be in the offing. Thicke sighed.

'Colverson!' he bellowed once again.

'Yes, Sarge?' A tall, wiry, dark haired constable appeared at Thicke's side.

'Where the hell have you been, lad?' Thicke growled.

'Taking statements, Sarge.'

'Taking statements!' Thicke spluttered, gesturing at the heaving mass of rancid humanity that elbowed each other aside as they tried to claim their just reward. 'You really think this lot have anything useful to say?' Thicke demanded. 'Bloody Gazette. As if we don't have enough work to do without the public telling us who we should be arresting. That's a copper's job that is, not something for all and sundry to have a go at.

'We don't need some sozzled tuppeny whore complaining that the Ripper's some foreign sailor who's come straight off the boat with a cleaver in his hand and is having a go at respectable whores when all she's really moaning about is not getting her fair share of his cash because she's too raddled for even a rancid matelot to give her a second look.'

Thicke's tirade seemed to have exhausted him and he stood there, red faced and breathing hard, staring intently at nothing.

'You never know, Sarge. Any small detail may be

important,' Colverson replied calmly.

Just then a voice from the back of the crowd rang out.

'In the name of Almighty God, heed my warning, for demons walk amongst us!'

Thicke groaned. 'Not him again. He's a bleedin' nutter. Thinks blood sucking demons are tupping the dollymops in Whitechapel.'

A thin, bespectacled cleric with dark, curly hair and a threadbare frock-coat had made his way in from the street and was haranguing those assembled masses. Raising his Bible high and his voice even higher to be heard above the babble of voices, he intoned: 'The Lord God has sent a plague amongst us to punish us for our sins.'

Sergeant. Thicke growled and shook his shaggy head. 'Take over the desk, Colverson,' he said, 'whilst I deal with this barmpot.'

PC Colverson obediently stepped into Sergeant. Thicke's place as Thicke lifted the counter flap and began to force his way through the crowd. The preacher continued his harangue.

'Demons live amongst us!' he shouted. 'Hiding in plain sight, despoiling innocent women and spreading their evil. Sinners give them succour and for the sake of their souls must be delivered to the Lord for judgement.' Seeing Thicke plowing a path towards him like a vengeful frigate fighting a tempestuous sea, he took a huge breath, the better to continue his sermon before his inevitable ejection from the premises. 'I will wield the burning sword of God in his service even as Leviticus tells us it must be so.'

'You!' Thicke bellowed, at last closing upon his quarry. 'Take your flamin' sword and get out of my station, sharpish.'

'Do not close your eyes to sin,' the priest intoned. 'For it shall surely overtake us all if left to flourish.'

'Out, I said,' Thicke shouted, seizing the preacher's arm, thrusting it painfully behind his back and shoving the shouting man of the cloth out the door and onto the pavement. 'And stay out!' Thicke instructed. Turning back, he brushed the dust of religious fervour from his hands. 'Bloody lunatic,' he muttered. 'Comes in here every day, blathering on about demons and sin, as if I haven't got enough to cope with.' He paused and looked around at the crowd of petitioners who had momentarily ceased their clamour to watch the entertainment. 'And you lot!' Thicke shouted. 'Clear off, the lot of you. There's no reward money being handed out to the likes of you, not now, not ever, so bugger off. Go on. Out!'

Reluctantly, the mob of hopefuls began filing out the door. Thicke stomped his way back behind the counter. 'If anyone wants me,' he told Colverson, 'I'll be having a cup of tea and I don't want to be disturbed unless it's urgent. Understood?"

'Understood, Sarge,' Colverson said, trying but not wholly succeeding in suppressing a smile. As his superior officer stomped his way to the station scullery for a brew and a snifter no doubt, the bedraggled priest crept silently back through the door through which he had unceremoniously just been ejected. Casting fearful glances from side to side he approached the counter once more. In a much quieter, pleading voice, he once again made his bid for understanding.

'Please,' he said. 'You must hear me out. I'm not mad. This is a menace that threatens our very souls.'

Colverson looked around him. Sergeant Thicke was nowhere in sight and the station was, momentarily at least a haven of peace and quiet. 'Just give me a second, 'he said. 'I'll find someone to take over the desk and then you and me can go and have a nice, quiet chat and you can tell me all about it. How does that sound?'

The troubled cleric took PC Colverson at his word and gave chapter and verse of the terror that faced the city as he saw it. PC Colverson meticulously transcribed his words into a report that he would later submit to his superior officer, Detective Chief Inspector Abberline. It seemed preposterous, but, as Inspector Abberline was fond of saying, perspective is paramount and any small detail many be important. It was a creed that PC Colverson strove to live by.

PRESENT DAY

1

The all-night launderette shed the only grubby light in an otherwise darkened street.

He was parked on the opposite side of the street, two shops down, beneath a conveniently blind street lamp. Not that one of those was hard to find in this neighbourhood.

He checked his watch. 1:15 a.m. Nearly twenty minutes since the last customers had entered. A small group. Two youths and an older man.

The three of them had approached together. Walking slowly past the lighted window of the Wash-a-Rama, glancing briefly inside.

They stopped outside a closed and shuttered newsagents to share a cigarette.

Threw the butt into the gutter.

Satisfied that no-one else had entered, they walked back, an increased sense of urgency in their stride.

They stepped inside and closed the door behind them.

The last one in had turned the shop sign to CLOSED.

He waited patiently, tapping his fingers on the steering wheel.

Then, a movement.

Shadows approaching the glass door.

The three men left the Wash-a-Rama, walking briskly.

He caught a snatch of conversation.

Too far away to make out any words.

They walked to the corner, paused briefly, then, as if at some unseen signal, walked off in different directions, swallowed quickly by the night.

He waited another five minutes.

Three cars went by.

None of them stopped.

No foot traffic.

Satisfied that it was as safe as it was ever going to get, he got out of the car, shut and locked the door behind him and stuffed the key into the front pocket of his jeans. He zipped up his windbreaker, stuffed his hands in his pockets and crossed the road.

As he approached the door, he could feel his heart speed up.

The sign still read CLOSED.

He peered inside.

Two rows of washers and dryers flanked a central aisle.

At the far end the aisle turned left, an area out of sight from the street.

That's where the girl must be.

He had seen her enter the Wash-a-Rama over an hour ago. She had no washing with her and she hadn't re-appeared.

There could be a rear exit he told himself, but if there was it was probably locked. Besides, if the girl wasn't there, what had those three guys been doing in there all that time?

He glanced quickly left and right.

No-one in sight.

He took a deep breath, held it for a second, then pushed open the door.

A bell rang as he entered, making his heart race even faster.

The noise elicited no response and he closed the door quietly behind him.

He moved quickly forward until he reached the end of the aisle.

He glanced to his left.

Almost opposite him was a door labelled Staff Only.

The rest of the alcove was taken up by three large dryers with a wooden bench facing them.

The girl sat, slumped, on the bench.

She was young.

Sixteen?

Seventeen?

Maybe as young as fourteen.

She had a mop of muddy blonde hair that fell forward, covering her face. She wore scuffed and stained Doc Martens, cut-off denim shorts and a denim jacket under which was a purple tee-shirt with the slogan "Rude when Nude" in black letters.

He watched her for a few seconds.

She was breathing heavily and every so often a small tremor made her limbs twitch.

Slowly, as though an invisible chain was keeping her gaze pinned to the floor, she raised her head and stared at him through the curtain of her hair.

'Hi,' she mumbled, her voice slurred and indistinct. 'Know what you want,' she said, laboriously. 'But can't.'

She stopped to lick her lips with a dry, smacking sound. ''m buzzin' too much already. Can't take no more.'

Her head lowered and came up again.

'Try Danielle over at the multi-storey. She'll see you right.'

Her head went down again and stayed down this time.

He moved forward and picked up one of her hands.

She made ineffectual flapping motions to try and pull away but finally gave up.

He stood up and let go of her hand. It sank back down to her lap in slow motion.

He reached into his pocket and pulled out a Stanley knife.

The sound of the blade clicking into position made the girl raise dull, disinterested eyes once more.

'I already told you, I'm all tricked out.'

Her head sank back and she slumped forward.

She would have fallen onto the tiled floor if he hadn't placed his hand on her chest and pushed her back until she leant against the wall.

She stared up at the ceiling, oblivious and uncaring about what happened next.

He moved forward and began cutting away her clothes.

When all her clothes had been reduced to tattered ribbons, he began cutting her flesh.

2

In his youth, DS Roy Pilkington had been nicknamed "Winklepicker" Roy, because of his fondness for pointed Italian-leather shoes. Over the decades that followed, his taste for that particular type of footwear diminished and so did his nickname.

Nowadays everyone just called him "Winkle".

Even the old lags whose collars he used to feel on a regular basis hadn't called him Mr Pilkington. It had always been: 'All right, Winkle, I'll come quietly.'

Not that Winkle had arrested anyone in...how long had it been?

Years.

Winkle had lost count.

Not since they had assigned him to the basement that ran the full length of Peel Street Station that's for sure. The ACC himself broke the bad news.

'We have a problem with the Central Repository for Archived Paperwork.'

'CRAP?'

'What? Oh, yes. A rather unfortunate acronym, not that it matters now. The place is riddled with asbestos apparently. Nobody can work there anymore so we're pulling it down. All the records are being shipped out to various stations throughout the country for assessment. Peel Street has to take its fair share and as we have a rather large basement, it's a rather large share I'm afraid. Unfortunately, the categorisation system has been rather lax over the years so the files are all a mite ...jumbled. Some go back over a hundred years so they have to be assessed for relevance and put forward for computerisation if deemed important enough. We need someone with experience and professional judgement to go through everything and weed out what we need to keep and what we can chuck out. That's why we need you, DS Pilkington.'

It was a life sentence, Winkle knew that. No way would they let him back out on the streets, but what choice did he have? He just got on with it, like he always had.

3

On his way in that morning, Winkle had loitered in the Incident Room. Something had happened, he could smell it in the air like ozone after a storm. People were moving with a sort of compressed energy like greyhounds waiting to be released from the traps. Conversation was terse, clipped, voices hushed and purposeful. White boards had been erected, empty now but that would change. It's always like this at the start, Winkle thought. Nothing to go on, no information except for the cold clay of the victim. Slowly, too slowly usually, the board would fill up, pieces of knowledge dredged up like silt, hoping for a few golden nuggets along the way. The tension in the air was palpable. The clock was ticking. Careers could be made and lost depending on the outcome, justice would be served if they did their job well, bitter recrimination and condemnation would be their lot if they did not.

'God, I miss this,' Winkle muttered.

Later, in his basement lair, Winkle withdrew a battered folder from his desk drawer. Mildewed and faded with age. It was one he knew well. A relic from a lost age. A collection of reports written by a young constable in the late 1800's. He'd read it a dozen times but something about it drew him back again and again.

Extract from the report of P.C. William Walter John Colverson, Whitechapel Station 9th November 1888
The victim was a street girl named Mary Jane Kelly. The body was discovered in a downstairs room in a lodging house at 13 Miller's Court by the landlord, one Stanley

Price, who raised the alarm. I was the first officer on the scene. The victim was naked and tied to the bed with coarse rope. A cloth gag had been placed in her mouth. The remains of her clothing was scattered upon the floor. The body was mutilated in a manner most horrific. Multiple lacerations covered the flesh from top to toe. I estimated over a hundred such wounds with particular attention being paid to the breasts and sex organs. Blood permeated the bed and the floor in copious quantities. In truth, I had never seen the like and hope never to again. It was a most hellish way to die.

Winkle shook his head. What must it have been like back then? No modern forensics, no computers, mobile phones, barely even fingerprints. All you had were your instincts and determination. That's real police work for you.

Winkle heard the rattle and clang of the freight lift as it crashed to a halt. The screech of the rusty doors as they were forced open and the protesting squeal as they were slammed shut again. He heard heavy footsteps advance on the concrete floor. Heard a thump and a muttered oath.

'Winkle!' a voice shouted. 'Where the hell are you?'

Winkle smiled to himself. 'Take a left, then second right and straight on till morning,' he said. After several seconds and several muttered curses, Detective Chief Inspector Cooper, a heavy set man in a lightweight suit, arrived at Winkle's desk.

'Bloody Hell, Winkle!' he said. 'It's like a bloody maze down here.' He gestured to the acres of stacked boxes and toppling paper. 'Is this lot safe?' he said.

'Don't know,' Winkle said. 'Had a chap from Health and Safety come down here once to assess it.'

'And?'

'I can still hear him sometimes. Over in that far corner, weeping quietly and moaning.'

'Very funny.'

'He doesn't think so. What can I do for you, Tommy? Only I've got an appointment later and I don't want to be late.'

'An appointment? You?' Cooper said.

'Yes, me. So what's up or is this just a social call?'

Cooper ran a finger round his collar, looking uncomfortable. 'No, it's business. Can't stay long, we've got a nasty one upstairs. Poor little cow got herself sliced up like a salami in a launderette of all places.'

'Wash-a-Rama?'

'How did you know?'

'Lucky guess. Phil the Greek's brother owns it. Phil used to run it as a knocking shop at night. Got one of his boys to mind the door and take the money from the punters as they went in. Cut out the middle man, see? Only a matter of time before something went tits up.'

'It did that all right, but Phil the Greek had nothing to do with it. He's doing six months for assault.'

'Really? I didn't know. They grow up so fast these days.'

Cooper grunted and took an envelope from his inside pocket. 'You've got a letter,' he said, and placed the envelope on the table in front of Winkle. 'It's from HRM.'

Winkle's eyebrows shot up. 'His Royal Majesty? Why would he be writing to me?'

He snapped his fingers. 'I know. It's that knighthood I applied for. I sent off the right number of box tops and everything.'

'Human Resources Manager,' Cooper muttered.

'Oh. That HRM.'

Winkle stared at the envelope for several seconds.

'Well?' said Cooper. 'Aren't you going to open it?'

'Why don't you tell me what it says?'

'How would I know? It's personal and private.'

'And they didn't send you a copy? How remiss of them.'

Cooper sighed and reached into his pocket again to pull out a single sheet of paper.

'All right,' he said. 'If that's how you want to play it.'

'I do. And don't bother with all the jargon. Just give me the bare bones.'

Cooper cleared his throat. 'You know you could have retired ten years ago, Winkle,' he said.

'Yes. I was aware. I was going to as well. Put in my papers and everything, but then…' he trailed off.

'But then your wife died.'

'Freda,' said Winkle softly.

'Yes, Freda. And at the time, the Chief Constable, Mr Marx…'

'Dear old Groucho. A true gentleman if ever there was one.'

'Yes, well, be that as it may, at the time, Mr Marx gave you special dispensation to stay on. Help take your mind off things as it were.'

'A noble gesture, much appreciated.'

'But it was only meant to be temporary, Winkle. A couple of months at most. Not a sodding decade.'

'I just kept turning up and they kept paying me. Nobody seemed to mind. I thought they'd forgotten about me'

'Well, they've remembered now. Human Resources may work with the speed of an arthritic tortoise, but even they figure out what's going on eventually.'

'And what is going on, Tommy? Precisely.'

'You're an oversight, Winkle. Have been for ten years. But not anymore. With all these budget cuts they're desperate to save money.'

'So?'

'So, it's time to retire. No ifs or buts. They've resurrected your paperwork. You've got a birthday coming up next month. They've given you until then. But after that, you're retired.'

'Happy Birthday to me. I'm surprised they didn't wrap it in a red ribbon.'

'Come on, Winkle. You can't like being stuck down here all the time.'

'I'm doing very important work. Something only someone with experience and professional judgement can do,' he said, deadpan.

'Bollocks. We'll get a couple of bluebottles down here and have the place cleared in a fortnight. You know that as well as I do.'

Winkle sighed. 'I suppose.'

'Come on. It's not that bad. Get out of here, Winkle. You've done your time and more. Go and get a life.'

'Doing what?'

'I don't know. Anything. Go on holiday. Climb a mountain. Scuba diving. Anything you fancy. Just live for a change.'

'Thanks for letting me know, Tommy.'

'We'll talk later. Organise a bit of a "do", eh?'

'Sure. Why not?'

Cooper turned and made his halting way back to the lift with only three wrong turns. Winkle stared at the white envelope, so clean and pristine amongst all the mouldering pulp, as he listened to the clangs and rattles of the lift as it groaned its way up to daylight.

4

Abigail Potter was his first. They were playing on the swings in the garden. He pushed. Abigail laughed and squealed with delight.

'Harder, harder!' she said. 'Push harder. Make it go higher.'

So he did.

'Harder, harder!'

And he pushed harder still.

'Harder, harder!'

And then it happened.

He knew what he was going to do.

What he had to do.

He knew what the likely outcome would be.

He did it anyway.

As the swing came back, he took a deep breath, reached up and shoved with all his might.

But he didn't aim for the swing.

He shoved Abigail in the small of her back as hard as he could. The swing twisted awkwardly. Abigail's screams of delight choked off into a startled squawk as she lost her grip. He watched as she took flight like some ungainly bird. Saw her plummet to the ground, face first, with a soft thumping sound. There was a moment of almost religious silence and then Abigail started to scream.

When concerned parents came running to see what the problem was, they found him straddling her, his face pressed close to hers. At first, they thought he was kissing her.

But he wasn't.

He was lapping at the blood that spurted from her broken nose. Licking it up, slurping it in, tasting it, swallowing it, his nose, lips and chin dripping red.

His mother dragged him up by his arm, hauled him to one side and crushed him to her as the other parents screamed and shouted and fussed over Abigail. 'Not like your father,' his mother whispered. 'You will not be like your father.'

His mother beat him that night.

Beat him with his dead father's leather belt.

Beat him to drive the Devil out of him.

Another first.

It would not be the last.

5

Not that anyone would notice, but Winkle was absent from his basement lair. He had an appointment to attend. An appointment. That was an understatement, but at least Tommy hadn't pressed him for details.

The middle-aged nurse who escorted Winkle into the examination room took a seat against the far wall where she could view him from the most unflattering angle.

The young woman who was operating the equipment was dough faced and stern. She glanced in Winkle's general direction then sniffed and turned her attention to the knobs and dials in front of her, the medical equivalent of kicking the tyres.

The Urologist, young enough to be Winkle's daughter, or possibly his granddaughter, introduced herself as Marie Coburn. Winkle lay on the examination table, naked from the waist down except for his socks. His big toe was poking through a hole in one of them and he told himself it was that alone which was making him blush.

Marie Coburn moved down the table. He felt her take hold of him gently in her rubberised fingers.

'I'm just going to pull back the foreskin,' she said.

Winkle nodded, not trusting his voice at this point and wondered if a degree of tumescence would make the exam more difficult or painful. In the end he needn't have worried on that score.

'I'm just going to apply some antiseptic gel,' Marie Coburn said. 'It might sting a bit.'

She did.

It did.

Winkle grunted.

'Just inserting the camera now,' she told him. 'You may feel a bit of pressure.'

She did.

He did.

Another grunt.

Winkle held himself as still as possible lest any movement should make the intruding apparatus veer off-course with disastrous results.

Marie Coburn finished the exam and tidied up after herself. As she was in the general vicinity, she told Winkle to roll over so that she could shake hands with his prostate, then told him he could sit up.

Winkle perched on the edge of the table and adjusted the folds of the hospital gown they had given him to wear to preserve his modesty, though why and from whom at that point he wasn't sure, but it seemed the right thing to do.

He cleared his throat. 'Well?' he said. 'What's the verdict?'

'Hmmm,' said Marie Coburn.

It was that "Hmmm" that sent shivers down Winkle's spine. Had she wanted to perform the exam now, he felt reasonably sure she would have had trouble finding the target area.

'I think we need to make you an appointment with the consultant,' she said. Winkle felt the blood drain from his face. The last time someone had said those words they had been speaking to his wife, Freda, and Winkle was well aware of how that had turned out.

The middle-aged nurse escorted Winkle back to the changing room. He dressed and made his way back into the daylight.

Dead man walking he thought.

6

These days Winkle was a creature of habit. Not all of them savoury, but routine had been his world for as long as he could remember and he saw no reason to change now.

Every Tuesday, Winkle visited a Chinese prostitute called Peggy Li.

'Not Peggy Lee the singer,' she'd told him when they had first met. 'Peggy Li the Hong Kong good time girl.'

And she'd laughed, a musical, embarrassed giggle that made Winkle smile every time he thought about it.

Not that Winkle made a habit of visiting prostitutes.

A bit of a conflict of interest there you might say, given his profession, but it had been his wife's idea.

Sort of.

It had been towards the end, that calm eye inside the hurricane of emotion that had engulfed them and swept them away, when all hope had finally been extinguished and only resigning yourself to the inevitable remained to provide what meagre comfort it may. They had been sitting on the sofa, not speaking, as if the silence could make it all go away. Freda had taken his hand and squeezed it with all her might.

He could barely feel it. Like a cobweb brushing against his skin.

'I don't want you to be lonely,' she had whispered. 'When I'm gone, I want you to go out and find someone. Someone who can make you happy. Promise me you will.'

Winkle promised.

At that point he would have promised her the world on a silver platter if she'd asked him for it.

Two days later, she was gone.

Winkle didn't think about that conversation again for several weeks.

Weeks in which he'd barely left the house except to attend the funeral.

Weeks in which the pile of takeaway cartons formed an ever growing mountain on the dining room table.

Weeks in which every cup, spoon, plate, knife and fork found their way into the kitchen sink, but none of them had seen a drop of water.

Weeks in which every drop of alcohol in the house had been consumed, the empty bottles overflowing the much put-upon dustbin.

Winkle simply woke up one morning, looked at the gathering detritus of his life and said to himself:

'Freda wouldn't want this.'

And he set to.

Tidying up, cleaning, polishing, washing, shopping.

It was as he was putting the last of the groceries away that he remembered their conversation.

He tried to ignore it, but it kept nagging at him.

He knew she was right.

Solitary by nature, taciturn and sarcastic by design, Winkle had few social skills.

He hadn't needed them.

That was Freda's department.

For thirty years she had been his rock, the sole purpose of his existence, he never wanted nor needed anyone else.

Until now.

But how to go about it?

Too old for disco's, he told himself.

Too scruffy and too poor for casino's.

Too scared for on-line dating – too many weirdo's.

So, how to go about it?

The answer, when it came, was startlingly simple, if deeply flawed.

When you want to learn to drive, he told himself, you take lessons from a professional driving instructor.

When you want to have a relationship with a woman, you practice on a professional whose job it is to boost your confidence and who is paid to like you no matter what.

Just temporary, he promised himself.

Just until I get up enough nerve to try it on a civilian.

And that is when Winkle started combing the small ad columns for escorts.

Of course, they were expecting him to have sex with them.

He never told them he was a copper and they would have been suspicious if he'd refused.

But things did not go well on the carnal front.

His first encounter left him confused and nervous.

Her name was Avril, a buxom blonde with a small scar above her right eye.

As he watched her undress, Winkle couldn't believe what he was seeing.

When did pubic hair go out of fashion? he asked himself.

It just wasn't natural.

And it wasn't just Avril.

The next three were the same.

Bald as an egg between their legs.

It made them seem too naked, too vulnerable, too...alien.

And when he saw his first piercing he nearly bolted for the door.

He couldn't perform and he couldn't tell them why.

He was about to give up and slouch back into an existence

of slovenly solitude when he saw Peggy's advert.

Discrete Asian lady offers personal
service to mature gentlemen.

There was a phone number and Winkle decided to give it one last try.

Peggy lived in a small semi on a quiet road in a respectable neighbourhood.

She met him at the door wearing a silk kimono and when she smiled, Winkle felt his nerves melt away.

The real test of course was still to come.

He remembered sitting on the side of her bed, watching as she slowly untied the sash of her kimono.

She turned her head slightly to one side, as though embarrassed at her own behaviour as she slowly slipped the gown from her shoulders, letting it drop to the floor, unveiling herself to him.

Winkle took in the smooth, ivory skin, the straight, jet black hair that fell to her waist, the delicate upturned breasts with the dark, protruding nipples, the flat belly and slim waist, but most of all, nestling between firm, but shapely thighs was a nest of neat, black hair.

And not a piercing or tattoo in sight.

Winkle sighed.

It was like coming home.

After that, it had become a regular event.

They didn't always have sex.

Sometimes they just talked or watched TV, just like a real couple.

It's just business, Winkle kept telling himself.

I'm paying her to like me.

It's just temporary, until I get up enough confidence to try my luck in the real world.

But it didn't seem like business.

It didn't seem temporary.

Unless you call nearly a decade of Tuesday afternoon's temporary.

What it was, was comfortable.

Winkle had found a safe haven and he was in no hurry to change.

He sat now, in Peggy's bed, in his vest, pants and socks, dunking a ginger nut in his tea as Peggy moved around the room, picking up his discarded clothes and folding them neatly.

'It's a bloody disgrace,' he said. 'I'm twice the copper these new fast track brown-nosers are and they're just kicking me to the side like a worn out shoe.'

Not that it would make any difference in the long run, he thought. I'm heading for the knackers yard one way or the other. But he didn't say that. Couldn't bring himself to say the word: Cancer. It wasn't Peggy's problem. He couldn't bear the thought of her feeling sorry for him and so he kept quiet.

'But you hate your job,' Peggy said, folding Winkle's creased and faded corduroys into a semblance of neatness. 'You always saying it a waste of your time.'

'Well,' said Winkle, 'it is, but there are some interesting cases down in that basement. And there's one copper in particular, back in Victorian times. Police Constable William Walter John Colverson his name was. He got involved in some really unusual cases. And he wrote it all down. Proper notebooks in them days, not these "tablets" and "laptops". There was a real copper for you. I'm thinking about writing a book about him when I retire. Give me something to do. And it's not just him. These files go back to the year dot and I've been absorbing all the investigative know-how of over a hundred years' worth of top coppers. I'm like a human storehouse of police tactics and skill. I'm like a coiled spring, just waiting to explode.'

He finished his tea, placed the cup and saucer (it was always a delicate bone china cup and saucer with Peggy, never a mug) on the bedside table and brushed crumbs from his vest.

A large ginger tom cat sat curled up comfortably by his side.

This was Chairman Meow, Peggy's constant companion.

'He was little ball of fluff when I first got him,' she had told Winkle. 'He could fit into one hand easy.'

Times had certainly changed.

Now, the Chairman was overweight and anti-social. His belly hung almost to the ground and woe-betide any unwary newcomer who dared to stray into his territory.

Winkle and the Chairman had hit it off right from the start.

Winkle reached out and tickled the ginger monster under the chin.

He purred like a jet plane waiting to take off.

Peggy finished folding Winkle's shirt and placed it on top of his trousers.

She hung his jacket on the hook behind the door and placed his shoes neatly under the bed.

Then, she moved smoothly and delicately into Winkle's line of sight, toying with the sash of her kimono as she turned her face shyly away from his gaze.

Winkle felt his heart beat faster.

It was always the same.

A ritual unveiling for his pleasure.

Ever since that very first time, Peggy had performed for him, just like this, sensing that it was somehow special and important to him to see her unadorned body in all its natural glory.

She slipped the silk from her shoulders, feeling a delightful shiver as is slipped down her back.

She paused, naked, letting him drink her in with his eyes.

It was something he never got tired of.

Winkle had never been rude enough to ask Peggy her age, but ten years had done nothing to diminish her beauty.

She was still as trim and firm and smooth in all the right places as she had been all those years ago, and if there was maybe a strand or two of silver in her ebony hair, it only added to her allure.

Winkle licked his lips.

Peggy waved her hand and the Chairman waddled to the side of the bed and launched himself to land with a thud and a disgruntled meow on the floor.

Peggy climbed onto the bed and snuggled down into the crook of Winkle's arm.

She kissed him softly on the lips and reached across him, slipping her arm beneath the waistband of his shorts.

As she did so, Winkle saw a plaster on her forearm.

He frowned.

It seemed to be a frequent occurrence these days, some small injury or blemish. It worried him.

'What have you done there?' he asked.

She looked at it as though seeing it for the first time.

'Oh, that. It's nothing. I just get clumsy sometimes. Opening a tin of cat food maybe.'

'Funny place to cut yourself opening a tin of cat food. It's not one of your clients is it? He's not roughing you up is he? Because if he is...'

'Shhhh.'

Peggy tilted his face towards her and kissed him again, more deeply this time, her tongue snaking into his mouth, her hand reaching further into his shorts.

Winkle groaned.

'There's my nice big policeman's truncheon,' she whispered, and giggled.

She worked him free of his underwear and slid down the bed.

He felt her warm breath and the tip of her darting tongue, her expert fingers caressing and arousing him.

He closed his eyes and abandoned himself, all copper's instincts forgotten, all curiosity abandoned.

If there was anything wrong, she'd tell me, he decided.

It was a decision Winkle would regret for the rest of his life.

7

It was a good night for listening to dead men sing. Leonard Cohen wanted it darker. David Bowie was a cracked actor and Jim Croce failed once again to save time in a bottle.

Winkle sat and listened. It wasn't a death sentence, Winkle knew that. Even if they found something wrong, these days they could work miracles. Surgery. Drugs. Chemo. Winkle shuddered. The very word made him go weak at the knees. It wasn't for him. If his time was up, so be it.

Later, he sat nursing a pint and brooding at his usual table in The Bull. One thing Winkle had always been good at was drowning his sorrows. His hospital visit and the news of his impending retirement sat heavily on his shoulders like the raven of doom and the Bull seemed the ideal place to contemplate his future. What there was of it anyway. It was an old fashioned pub.

No wide screen telly.

No spritzers.

Dark wood and smoke stained ceiling.

It suited him.

The door opened and Winkle glanced up idly. The Bull's usual clientele were male, middle aged or older and monosyllabic. The newcomer was female, slightly overweight, dressed in a blue duffel coat and had the look of someone who could be decidedly chatty.

Bloody hell, Winkle thought, who let Paddington Bear out?

She paused and looked around the room.

The room looked back.

She saw Winkle and gave a small nod.
Winkle raised his eyebrows.
He didn't recognise her.
He shrugged and went back to his pint.
A few seconds later, a voice said: 'Can I join you?'
He looked up to see the duffel coated intruder standing next to him with a glass of something that looked suspiciously non-alcoholic in her hand.
He glanced around the room.
Plenty of empty tables.
Why does she want to sit here? he wondered.
Maybe it's a joke, he thought.
Maybe the lads at the station have organised an early strippergram for my retirement.
She didn't look like a strippergram.
Forties, he guessed, with mousy hair, blue eyes and just a hint of make-up.
He shrugged. 'If you like,' he said.
She smiled and sat down.
Winkle watched her warily.
She leaned forward.
'I'm Nancy,' she said.
'How do you do,' Winkle replied.
She looked at him as if expecting more, then, after a moment, she said, quietly:
'I know what you need.'
A tart!
No way.
'Do you?' he said.
'Yes.'
'What might that be?'
She looked around.

Nothing had changed.

Nothing had changed in The Bull since 1945, but she didn't look like she wanted to take any chances.

'Not here,' she said. 'Meet me in the alley in five minutes.'

'All right.'

She stood up, left her untouched drink and went out of the door.

Winkle didn't want to do it, she seemed a nice woman, but this sort of blatant soliciting was bound to get her into trouble at some time if it hadn't already. She didn't look like a professional. Winkle prided himself on having a nose for spotting working girls a mile off. Probably some poor housewife whose husband had done a bunk and was short on the rent. Thought this was a quick and easy way to get out of arrears. All the while promising herself it would only be this once. Maybe a couple at most. But it never stopped at just a couple. Whatever her problem, this was definitely not the answer. It was her lucky day that she chose him, he thought. Better him than some "Jack the Lad" who'd give her a right going over for her trouble.

I won't arrest her, he thought. I seem to have lost the knack of arresting people these days. A stern talking to should do the trick.

Winkle downed his pint and followed the duffel coat.

A fine drizzle had started since Winkle had entered the pub. He pulled the collar of his coat up and trudged around the corner into the alley.

Miserable way to make a few bob, Winkle thought. Giving wrinklies a cheap thrill behind the dumpsters in the rain. There were no lights in the alley and, at first, Winkle thought he had been stood up. Then he thought that maybe this was all a con. The duffel coat was just to lure him outside where her beefy boyfriend was waiting to mug him.

His steps faltered.

There was a time when he would gleefully have played along and given the good for nothing mugger a bloody good hiding before marching him down to the station. But that was long ago, when he was in his prime. Too long ago, he decided. And these days, even litter louts seemed to carry Uzi's.

He was about to turn tail when a shadow detached itself from the wall, further down the alley.

'I'm here,' she whispered.

Winkle looked behind him.

No beefy boyfriend was in evidence.

The alley led through to the next street and in the dim streetlight it looked deserted apart from Winkle and the Paddington lookalike.

Against his better judgement, Winkle decided to keep to his original plan.

She looked a nice woman, he told himself. Put a bit of a scare into her, a bit of a talking to, maybe give her the price of a cuppa and send her on her way.

Do policemen really do that sort of thing these days? he wondered.

Probably not, he decided, but then, I'm barely a policeman anymore, so what the hell.

He trudged towards the sound of her voice. She was well positioned. Half way down the alley where the shadows were darkest, furthest away from the street lights at either end. He could make out her pale face, framed by the hood of her duffel coat. She smiled.

'Good,' she said. 'I knew I was right about you.'

Winkle cleared his throat. 'There's something I need to tell you,' he said.

'You don't need to say anything,' she said. 'Just relax. You're in safe hands.' And she pulled something from her coat pocket. Even in the almost non-existent light, Winkle could see the pale glint of steel.

'Hell's teeth!' he muttered and stepped back, his foot skidding on a discarded tin can he almost lost his balance until the opposite wall met his back and steadied him.

Maybe this is what they call girl power, he thought. She doesn't need a beefy boyfriend, she does the mugging herself!

She moved closer to him. 'Don't worry,' she said. 'I know what I'm doing.'

'So do I,' Winkle muttered, 'and I'm not sure I like it!'

She laughed softly. 'You are funny,' she said. 'Anyone would think you'd never done this before.'

Done what? he thought. Pissed myself in a back alley because some menopausal girl scout waved a pig sticker under your nose? Some big brave policeman you are.

Before Winkle could gather his thoughts, the woman stepped back. 'We have to be quick,' she said, 'before someone sees us.' She pushed the sleeve of her duffel coat up and held out her arm for him to see. 'See,' she said, 'no marks. You're the first in a while.'

'Lucky me,' Winkle rasped.

What the hell is she on about? he thought.

And then she brought the knife up, a silver blur in the shadows, and brought it down in a quick, decisive slash across her own arm. She took a deep breath and held her bleeding arm up to his face. 'Don't take too much,' she said. 'I may need to minister to others tonight.'

For several seconds, Winkle stood, frozen, against the

wall. He watched as droplets of blood trickled down the woman's arm and fell to the ground. He has a sneaking suspicion that some of them were splashing on his shoes. Finally, he said:

'What the bloody hell are you playing at? You'll get gangrene you daft cow!'

The woman's face crumpled into a look of confusion and then embarrassment. She stepped back. 'Oh, no,' she said. 'You mean you're not... Oh, I am so sorry. I didn't mean...Forgive me.'

And then she turned and ran.

Winkle listened to her footsteps fade into the night.

It was a full five minutes before he could prise himself away from the wall and stagger into the street.

What just happened? he wondered.

As he turned his steps homeward, he tried to tell himself it had all been a dream, some product of his overwrought imagination.

But he knew it wasn't.

I don't have that good an imagination, he told himself.

8

Religion came into his Mother's life soon after Abigail Potter.

The church smelt damp and musty but it was better than the endless hours of kneeling and praying she had subjected him to at home.

She had explained about the Mass. How the Liturgy of the Eucharist, the receiving of the body and blood of Christ into his own body, would save him.

The only word he heard was "blood".

The service was long and solemn. It bored him, but then, as he joined the line of supplicants, his Mother's guiding hand upon his shoulder, his heart began to race. If all these people were like him, if all of them were eager to experience the taste of blood, then surely he could not be as terrible as his Mother had made out?

Slowly the line shuffled forward.

When it came to be his turn, his Mother gave him a gentle shove. He knelt and gazed up at the Priest. The Priest spoke some words but he didn't hear them. All he could focus on was the wafer that the man dipped into the chalice. It came up stained red. The Priest offered it to him. Trembling, he opened his mouth. He tasted the sweat on the man's fingers as he placed it on his tongue. He closed his mouth and closed his eyes expecting ecstasy but finding ... nothing.

Worse than nothing. This was not blood. He knew the taste of blood. This was sour and dull, not sharp and sweet the way Abigail Potter's blood had tasted as it tricked down his throat.

He had been cheated. Mother had promised him this

would be the answer to all his prayers and instead it was foul and rancid on his tongue.

He tried to chew, tried to swallow, but he couldn't. His chest began to heave. He was aware of movement, murmured voices all around him, his Mother's hand upon his shoulder, urging him to stand, but it was too late for that.

With a convulsive shudder, her spat the foul not-blood out of his mouth. It landed with a soft splat on the Priest's white vestment. He heard the gasp of horror and alarm that went up from those watching. Heard the babble of voices, rising in righteous anger, following them down the aisle as his Mother dragged him out of the church never to return.

And he smiled.

The smile lasted until they got home. The door had hardly slammed shut behind them before she began flailing at him with her fists, screaming, her face puce with anger.

'You're an abomination!' she screamed. 'An abomination just like your father. He had a devil inside him and you have a devil inside you and you're both going to hell!'

It was the first time he had heard that word. Abomination. It would not be the last. Much later, when the pain had subsided, he looked it up in the dictionary.

abomination: *Someone or something that causes great revulsion or abhorrence.*

So that is what I am, he thought. And the idea settled in his mind like a roosting bird. But that was later. After his Mother had dragged him upstairs. After she had stripped him naked the better for him to suffer his penance. After she had fetched his dead father's belt. After she had whipped him raw. After his screams had melted into muffled sobs and the sobs to grunts, the silence broken only by her ragged breathing.

Such was the nature of their worship from that moment on. Private. Painful. Relentless. And pointless. His Mother thought the beatings kept the devil at bay. It just kept it hidden. There was a difference.

9

Dolly Boone was flustered. It happened now and then but not often. Maybe it was the weather putting her psychic antenna out of whack. She was nowhere near the psychic that her Aunt Edna was of course. Aunt Edna had been chatting to the spirits ever since she was a girl. She had taught Dolly how to let her mind slip into another rhythm, to focus on what was not visible as opposed to what was. Hard though she tried, Dolly had never had a bona fide spiritual experience. Her talent was more muted, more low key than that. She was sensitive to other people's vibrations. It hadn't helped with Trevor of course. He had definitely slipped under her radar and she had paid a hard price for that, but she had been young and in love, or so she thought, and she had ignored all the warning signs. But now, things were very different. Her psychic skills enabled her to home in on those in need of her services. Their aura, usually bright and glowing, was darker, harder to see and Dolly was always right. Except tonight. It happens, she told herself. The terminally ill have similar auras. There are subtle differences but it's an easy mistake to make.

'That poor man,' Dolly muttered, as she dabbed TCP onto the unused and unwanted cut on her arm. I wonder if he knows? Maybe I should go back, try to find him, tell him to get help. But how to explain? He'd think I was mad. Whoever he was, he was not long for this world and nothing could change that. But he deserved to know. Yes, I have to find him again, Dolly decided, and let him know if he doesn't already.

Her decision made, Dolly shrugged off the night's

memories as, wrapped in her fluffy blue bathrobe, she stood in front of the full length mirror fixed to the wardrobe door, her skin still moist from her bath. Inspecting the troops she called it. She gave her reflection a wry grin, loosened the belt on her robe, shrugged it from her shoulders and let it fall to the floor. Now she faced the world, and herself, naked. It was an act of bravado that still made her shiver after all these years. Nothing hidden, no deceptions, physical or emotional. It was an honest and pure act that defined her as a person and had become as much a part of her life as breathing.

She started at the top.

Hair. Needs cutting. Used to be a dirty blonde – didn't we all – now it's just a muddy brown with grey streaks. Call it highlights and leave it at that.

She raised her arms above her head. A few more years before the bingo wings were ready for take-off.

Her hands were square with blunt fingers, which was acceptable given her job.

Tits. Like two half-filled hot water bottles that pointed each side of her navel. Long nipples and large areola. She hated her nipples. In the dim, distant past when her breasts were firm and forward facing, the boys had liked chewing on them well enough and nowadays nobody saw them anyway.

Dolly sighed and pulled herself out of her reverie and carried on with her inspection.

She slapped her belly and watched the fat wobble. Not quite on the Richter scale yet.

Personal grooming was a warped fad as far as Dolly was concerned and an unruly nest of dark hair poked out from beneath her gut.

Her legs were sturdy and too short for her frame but her mini-skirt days were long past.

Feet. Everyone had ugly feet, but at least they were clean and the nails polish free. Painted toe-nails were hideous and cheap.

She turned and peered over her shoulder. When her ass was big enough to rest a pint pot on she'd start to worry.

Cellulite had invaded her thighs but that was only human nature, right?

Love handles like a cabin trunk, but her shoulders were nice, if a little wide.

Inspection finished she picked up her robe and shut the wardrobe door.

Her pale blue uniform was hanging up behind the bedroom door, newly washed with the smell of warm ironing. It gave her an inner glow of pride every time she put it on. Care Assistant. That's what she was and that was a worthwhile thing to be. The retirement home she worked in was nice and airy and the people there were cheerful and grateful. A meaningful life well lived, that was what she told herself she had and that was all anyone could ask for.

Dolly slipped into her comfy nightdress, the one with pictures of kittens on it and set the alarm clock. She had a full day tomorrow and didn't want to be late. It would never do to keep the Sir Francis waiting.

10

Chairman Meow was waiting on Winkle's doorstep when he got home.

When he saw Winkle make his way up the path, he gave a deep, loud meow and came trotting towards him, bumping into Winkle's legs and rubbing his face against his trousers.

'Chairman?' Winkle said. He bent down and rubbed the ginger tom behind the ears. 'What are you doing here?' he asked. Until now, Winkle had only seen the Chairman at Peggy's. 'How did you know where I lived?' he said. The cat responded by purring loudly and pushing against Winkle's legs hard enough to knock him over. He straightened up. 'Well,' Winkle said,' it's nice to see you, but there's a hot toddy with my name on it in there, so off you go and do whatever it is your sort does at night.'

Winkle moved towards his front door, but the cat wound itself between his feet almost tripping him, his meow escalating to a raucous screech of annoyance.

'Look, old son,' Winkle told him as he fumbled for his key, 'I've had a bad day, all right? I'll see you next week as usual. Now scram.'

But the cat stayed. Reached up on his hind legs and sank his claws into Winkle's leg.

'Ow!' Winkle stepped back. The cat followed, darting forward and taking hold of Winkle's trouser leg in his teeth and tugging. As Winkle took a reluctant step forward to maintain his balance, the Chairman released his hold, trotted a few steps down the path, then darted back and repeated the manoeuvre.

Winkle stared at him. 'What?' he said. 'You want me to

follow you?'

The Chairman meowed at him in a tone that unmistakably said: 'At last! Why are you humans so slow on the uptake.'

Winkle scratched his head. 'I'll be blowed,' he muttered. 'Do you think you're a dog or something?'

The cat didn't answer, just trotted a few steps down the path, paused and looked back over his shoulder. Winkle sighed. 'All right,' he said. 'Why not? Today couldn't get any stranger. Go on then, where are we going?' He waved his hand and the cat moved smartly off. Winkle began to trudge reluctantly behind.

Winkle followed the Chairman through side streets and across main roads. The cat kept up a brisk pace despite his hefty bulk. Every so often he would look back over his shoulder. 'I'm coming, I'm coming,' Winkle puffed, the brisk pace seemingly more uncomfortable for him than his feline guide. So intent was Winkle on keeping the Chairman in sight, he lost track of where they were going. It wasn't until they reached their destination that Winkle realised where they were. He paused and wiped sweat from his brow.

'Here?' he said. 'You went through all that palaver just to get me to walk you home!' Winkle looked up at Peggy's familiar semi as the Chairman hurried towards the front door. 'Barmy bloody cat,' Winkle grumbled. 'And I'm even worse for falling for it.'

He was about to turn on his heel and head home once more, when a loud, screeching cry from the Chairman drew his attention.

'What now?' Winkle said as he turned back. The Chairman was sitting on the doorstep. Winkle blinked. It took him a second or two to realise there was something wrong with this picture.

The front door was open.

Peggy would never leave her front door open.

Winkle quickly scanned the rest of the house. Darkness. No lights in any of the windows. The downstairs curtains were open. Peggy religiously drew all her curtains at night, Winkle knew that for a fact. The curtains in the upstairs front bedroom were shut, but no light showed from behind them. Winkle felt his pulse quicken.

Something was definitely wrong here.

He moved forward at a lumbering trot. The Chairman disappeared inside the darkened house. By the time Winkle cautiously pushed open the front door and stepped over the threshold, the cat had disappeared upstairs. Winkle could hear the quick thud of his paws on the floorboards. There was no other sound apart from Winkle's booming heartbeat. He looked around. As near as he could tell in the gloom, everything looked normal.

Taking a deep breath he began to climb the stairs. 'Peggy?' he called softly. If she was up there, he didn't want to startle her. The front door hadn't been forced, so maybe the lock was faulty. Maybe she'd just forgotten to draw the curtains. Everybody gets forgetful some time or another. Winkle kept repeating the litany of maybe's as he reached the top landing. Peggy's bedroom door was open a crack. The Chairman sat patiently in the doorway. He looked over his shoulder at Winkle and then back at the bedroom door. Winkle nodded. 'All right, puss,' he said, 'you've got me here, now let's see what's going on.'

Slowly, Winkle inched his way along the landing. With the tip of one finger he gently pushed the door open. Taking another deep breath, he stepped inside. The streetlight from outside gave just enough illumination for him to see.

He stood, frozen. Nothing in all his years on the force had prepared him for this. Nothing ever could.

Peggy was naked on the bed. She lay on her back, her arms and legs tied to the bedposts with red cords. Dimly, Winkle realised that her bonds were strips of her red kimono, the remains of which lay crumpled on the floor. A further wad of the same material was wadded up and stuffed in her mouth.

To muffle her screams.

And she would have screamed.

Anyone would.

Her body was covered in cuts. Dozens, maybe hundreds of them. Everywhere. Her flesh was smeared crimson from head to toe. Most were superficial, Winkle realised, designed to hurt, but not kill. The blood spatter on the walls and ceiling were proof that at some point a major artery had been severed, but Winkle reasoned that this had intentionally been far on in the process. This had been a slow, cruel, agonising death. And she *was* dead, Winkle had no doubt about that. He could detect no rise and fall of her chest as she struggled for breath. He should check for a pulse, but he knew it was futile. The blood that soaked her body, the bed and the floor was congealed, indicating a fair passage of time. And so much of it. No human being could lose this much blood and survive.

A line from one of the reports he had been reading in his basement lair came unbidden into his mind. A report from the notebook of PC Colverson, written over a hundred years ago at the time of the Jack the Ripper murders:

It was a most hellish way to die.

A most hellish way to die. Winkle felt a pain in his chest and realised he had been holding his breath. As he exhaled, acid tears stung his eyes, his stomach began to rebel and he turned quickly, almost falling down the stairs in his haste. He made it out of the front door before falling on his hands and knees and vomiting.

11

Her name was Trixie.

She was younger than him, 21 or 22 maybe, and every fortnight she would come to cut Mother's hair. He used to look forward to her visits. He missed them now. Mother never liked going to a salon you see, too many people, too insanitary, but Trixie came to their house where Mother felt comfortable, safe and secure. Apart from Church, Mother rarely ventured out into the world. Somehow she had lost her taste for it over the years. He used to sit and watch as Trixie snipped and washed and curled Mother's hair. She had bright green eyes and a spray of freckles across her snub nose.

He thought he was in love. Mother had never allowed him to have a girlfriend. They inflamed his lust and lust fed the Devil inside him. They had no television because Mother said it showed nothing but brazen hussies parading their flesh. Most newspapers and magazines were banned because they contained nothing but images of violence and degradation. And no meat. Never any meat. Meat inflamed his urges and fed the Devil. A strict vegetarian diet, that was the only way.

He was on his way back from doing the supermarket shopping when he saw Trixie. He had loaded up his carrier bags and headed for the car park.

She was waiting for him when he got there, leaning against his car, smiling.

'Hello,' she said.

'Um, hello?' he replied, confused, scared, uncertain about what was happening. He felt the Devil stir. He blushed. She laughed but not unkindly.

'I've got a day off,' she said. 'Want to take me for a ride?'

'I've . . . got to get home.'

'That's okay. I'll come with you. If you want.'

He did want. He wanted that more than anything in his life. He nodded and she smiled again.

In the end it was as simple as that. She didn't seem to mind that he couldn't think of anything to say. She kept up a stream of innocuous chatter about her life, her friends, the people she worked with. It was all so normal for her, so utterly exotic for him.

As he pulled in to his driveway his heart began to hammer. Mother was at a Church meeting. They went on for hours. He knew the house was empty. He didn't even have to ask her in, she just assumed they would both go inside. She helped him carry his shopping inside. They placed the bags on the kitchen table but didn't unpack them. Instead, she put her arms around his neck and pulled him close, kissing him on the lips as she ran her hand through his hair. She tasted of peppermint and her lips were soft and moist. As she pressed her mouth against his he automatically opened his lips and her tongue slithered into his mouth. It was a strange, wet sensation and he eventually placed his hands around her waist. It was only when she slid her hand between his legs that he jumped back, startled. She grinned at him and licked her lips.

'I knew you'd be shy,' she said. She reached out and took hold of his hand. 'Come on,' she said. 'Which room is yours?'

He let her lead him upstairs, dumbly pointing out the door of his bedroom. Once inside she kissed him again. Then she stood back and started to undress. She did it quickly and with assurance. He could only stare, dumbfounded at her nakedness.

'Like what you see?'

He nodded.

'Well don't hang about,' she said. 'Let me help you.'

Her fingers were nimble and swift. It only took her seconds to strip him. Flustered, on the verge of panic, he felt ashamed and elated all at once. He blushed and cupped his hands over his genitals. She laughed again and sank down on her knees.

'Don't cover up the best bits,' she said and reached out to pull his hands away. He didn't resist. She studied him, her head tilted to one side.

'It's nice,' she said. 'Be even nicer when he grows up a bit.' And she leaned forward and took him into her mouth. He gasped. He thought he was going to faint, the blood was pumping so hard through his temples. He listened to the slurping, sucking sounds, felt her soft, wet tongue and her small, hard teeth. And then she stopped and he felt like his whole world had ended.

She stood up. 'That's more like it,' she said. A satisfied smile playing on those wicked lips. She reached out and tugged him towards the bed.

Many times afterwards he tried to remember exactly what happened next, what *she* did, what *he* did, the sights, the sounds, the scents, but he never could. It was all a jumble, a glorious confusion. He did think that it was possibly the greatest moment of his life, but the only thing he could remember clearly was the way it ended.

He was lying on his back, Trixie astride his hips, moving slowly up and down. He was inside her, his hands fondling her round breasts, her face contorted in what he thought at first was pain but later realised was lust. It was all so perfect.

And then the door opened. He turned his head lazily, distracted by the movement. Mother stood framed in the doorway, her face a mask of simmering hatred.

He tried to speak, to explain. He never got the chance. Mother screamed and launched herself forward. Trixie didn't know she was there until Mother smacked into her knocking her off of the bed, off of him, and onto the floor.

Both women were screaming then. Trixie from fear, Mother from righteous indignation. Mother grabbed a twin handful of Trixie's long hair and hauled her to her feet. Mother had momentum behind her and before Trixie knew what was happening, Mother had dragged her downstairs kicking and screaming to the front door. A final shove sent her out into the street. Naked. The door slammed shut behind her.

Screaming obscenities, Trixie smashed her fists against the wood demanding her clothes. As he heard Mother's measured tread coming up the stairs he gathered up Trixie's things and tossed them out of the window, all except one shoe which he found later under the bed. He just had time to see Trixie gather up her clothes, still screaming madly, as the door opened and Mother stood there once more. This time his dead father's belt dangled from one hand.

He knew what was going to happen and he submitted meekly to his chastisement, but this time it was worse than ever before. He whimpered, he screamed, he begged but the beating went on and on. He didn't know it had stopped. He hurt so much he could barely move, barely breathe.

Panting, groaning, he crawled onto his knees, his head hanging down, sweat dripping onto the carpet. When he finally had the strength to turn around he saw Mother. Not towering over him as he expected. Not readying herself for another onslaught. She was sitting on the floor, her back against the wall, her legs straight out in front of her. The belt lay coiled in her lap. Her right hand was clutching her left arm. Her mouth was open, her eyes staring. He crawled towards her, his hand reaching out to tentatively touch hers. He wanted forgiveness but he knew he wouldn't get it. He stared at his dead Mother's face and he began to weep.

12

'You want what?' DCI Cooper's voice cracked with incredulity and the sheer volume of his question.

Winkle drew himself up to his full height and smoothed down his wrinkled jacket. 'I want to be lead investigator on the case,' he demanded.

'Have you gone bloody mad?'

'I'm the most senior officer on the squad.'

'Only because you're older than God!'

'I have personal knowledge of the latest victim which could be invaluable.'

'You were shagging her!' Cooper screamed the accusation, making the windows of the cubicle that passed for his office rattle. 'And she was a prozzie!' he finished.

'You've got a serial killer on your hands,' Winkle countered. 'You need all the help you can get.'

'Not yet we haven't,' Cooper muttered. 'You know the rules. There has to be three. Enquiries will be pursued in tandem as per orders.'

'Bollocks!' Winkle offered. 'Look at the MO. That poor lass in the launderette and...' his voice choked, he swallowed and continued more quietly, '...Peggy. Their injuries were identical. It has to be the same bloke. He cuts them to buggery and then finishes them off by cutting their throats. It has to be a serial.'

'It doesn't matter,' Cooper told him through gritted teeth. 'You can't be involved in the case and that's that.'

'Each time he kills he's learning, getting more confident.'

'What if he is? The answer's still no. Winkle, for the last time, you're bloody lucky you're not the prime suspect! Not only can you not be involved in the case, you can't even be here. Bugger off home. You're on gardening leave until you retire. You can come back in for your leaving "do" but that's it. Until then I don't want to see hide nor hair of you anywhere near this investigation, is that clear?'

Winkle resisted the temptation to slam the cubicle door behind him as he left. Every pair of eyes in the squad room glanced in his direction as he emerged. Winkle straightened his tie and brushed invisible dust from his lapel. 'He's thinking about it,' he said as he walked, slowly and dejectedly towards the lifts.

Despite DCI Cooper's instructions, Winkle did not head straight home. Instead he took the freight elevator down to his basement hidey-hole. It was almost with a sense of sadness that he realised he might never be here again. He emptied files from a cardboard box and began collecting his pitifully few personal items. The pile of reports from the late lamented PC Colverson sat on his desk. On impulse, Winkle swept them into the box. No-one's going to miss them, he reasoned. And I really might write that book one day.

After I find the bastard who killed Peggy that is.

Winkle snuck out of the station with his illicit box like a thief in the night. No-one stopped him, no-one even noticed. They were all too busy. Despite what the rules said, they all knew they had a serial killer on their hands. Let them get on with it, Winkle thought. Let them use their computers and their internet searches. Some crimes could only be solved the old fashioned way. He had a feeling this was one of them.

13

They can keep their DNA and their CSI bollocks, Winkle thought to himself. Cases aren't solved in a test tube or on a computer screen, they're solved because someone talks. Faithful plods doing the rounds, shaking the trees, asking the right questions. Sometimes, people don't even know what they know. It's not until some copper's instinct puts two and two together that the case is cracked. Don't stint on the shoe leather, that's what Winkle's first inspector had told him and that's just what Winkle intended to do now. Pound the streets, talk to people, gather evidence, piece together all the tiny fragments of Peggy Li's life until he found a lead. And it all started in a greasy spoon just off the market.

The blonde was called Maggie. Mid-fifties, all fake fur, dark roots and glass diamonds. The skinny redhead was Julie. Pale, pock-marked face, the tattoos on her arms not quite hiding the old track marks. She chain smoked and drank too much but she was fighting it. Sandy was a brunette with three kids under ten and none of the fathers in evidence. Annie looked like someone's granny, silver haired and twinkly eyed. Winkle had never seen her without a ball of wool and knitting needles, always working on something unidentifiable. Amongst themselves they called themselves the Old Slappers Coffee Club. Most mornings about this time you could fine them in Big Len's having a cuppa and a chat. Peggy had introduced him to them. This was when Winkle and Peggy's relationship had slipped from professional into something else; Winkle didn't really have a name for it. Friendship, certainly. Domesticity even. He'd been moaning about needing new curtains as Peggy managed to tea-bag and carry on a conversation at the same time like the true practitioner of the erotic arts that she was. 'I take you shopping,' she said as she came up for air. Winkle had to think twice about whether it was wise to be seen in public together, but then, if wisdom had been a requirement, they would never have met in the first place. It was the first of many outings, "off the clock". And then, one day, she told him she was going to introduce him to her friends. That made Winkle go cold inside, but he had trudged along anyway for Peggy's sake. The "girls" as she called them were distant at first. The natural antipathy between working girls and serving police officers putting up an understandable barrier. But gradually, as Peggy chatted away, laughing and joking, the temperature thawed. Winkle had been accepted as an honorary member of their inner circle. It was the closest thing to friendship he had known for many years.

Maggie noticed him as he came through the door. She stood up, her high heels clattering on the worn lino, and came and threw her arms around his neck. She hugged him tightly and Winkle almost choked on her perfume. The thick layer of powder on her face tickled his nose and made him want to sneeze.

'How you holdin' up darlin'', Maggie whispered.

Winkle nodded into her shoulder. 'Just taking it one day at a time,' he said.

'Ain't we all, luv, ain't we all.'

'I need to do something. Not official. They're kicking me out, making me retire and even if they weren't, they wouldn't let me near the case. But I have to do something. It was Peggy,' he said plaintively. 'You were her closest friends. I thought you might know something.'

Maggie released him from the bear hug and looked up at him. 'You really...' she paused, afraid to utter the word that was on her lips. '...cared about her, didn't you?' she finished. Winkle nodded. Maggie sighed. 'Don't know what we can tell you, luv, but we'll do our best. For Peggy, eh?'

Winkle nodded again, too afraid to speak lest the effort trigger the tears welling up behind his eyes. Maggie squeezed his hand and led him to the table.

'You might want to wipe your nose,' she whispered. 'Bit of a dew-drop forming.' As Winkle fished an ancient handkerchief from his pocket and blew his nose loudly, Maggie gestured to the stocky aproned individual behind the counter. 'Tea all round, Len,' she called and he nodded.

Winkle took his seat. After the usual uncomfortable mutterings of consolation, Winkle said: 'Has anyone been around to speak to you yet?'

'Old Bill, you mean?' Maggie asked. Winkle nodded. 'Not yet. Only a matter of time I suppose.' They nodded agreement. Conversation paused as Len delivered five cups of tea. He put a beefy hand on Winkle's shoulder. 'On the house,' he said. 'She was a fine lady was Peggy.' Everyone nodded agreement and Winkle saw tears in the big man's eyes as he took up his place behind the counter once more.

They sipped their tea and continued to speak in low voices as the morning trade came and went around them.

'You expect it now and then,' Maggie said. 'In this business you always get the odd nutter.'

'But not like this.' Annie's needles clacked away as she spoke. 'This is above and beyond. I don't mind a bit of S & M, bit of bondage, role play, that sort of thing. But this is out of order.'

Winkle paused, his cup of tea half way to his lips as he stared at the small, plump figure peering at her knitting through gold rimmed spectacles. If nothing else, this morning was proving to be an education.

'And it's not just Peggy either,' Julie chipped in. 'There was that Charlene the other night, poor little mare, sliced up like a sausage.'

'Charlene?' Sandy asked.

'You know, Laundry Lil,' Maggie again.

'Oh, her. I know who you mean now.'

Maggie turned to Winkle. 'We called her Laundry Lil because she did most of her work out of an all-night launderette.'

'Daft place to work if you ask me,' Annie clack-clacked away.

'She had to give the owner a free blow job every Friday, but she reckoned it was worth it. Told me she did it because she could wash her clothes and work at the same time,' Sandy added. 'I went in there once to see how she was getting on and she was sitting there starkers except for a pair of boots, watching her clothes go round.'

'Least it's warm in a launderette,' Julie said. 'I remember one night last winter, must have been fifteen below, I had this punter who wanted to do it in the park, up against a tree. Nearly froze my nipples off and I got splinters in my arse.'

'You're lucky that's all you got in your arse!' Maggie said.

'Cheeky mare!'

Winkle tapped gently on the table. 'Ladies, ladies,' he said. 'Fascinating though this is, it's not getting us very far is it?'

Maggie: 'Sorry luv.'

Julie: 'Don't know what you expect us to tell you anyway.'

Annie: 'Lovely girl, Peggy. Didn't deserve to go like that.'

Sandy: 'No-one does. But we weren't there. We didn't see anything.'

Winkle drew in a deep breath. Witness statements were notoriously unreliable but he had nowhere else to start.

'You might not have seen the actual attack,' he said, 'but you know Peggy better than anyone. Did you notice anything different about her in the last few weeks? A change in her behaviour? Did she seem worried or frightened? Did she mention anyone, a name, someone new that you hadn't heard of before?'

Maggie: 'She bought herself a new jumper.'

Julie: 'Talked about going away on holiday. Greece or somewhere.'

Annie: 'She always talked about going on holiday. Never went though.'

Sandy: 'Thought about getting that cat of hers spayed. Said she saw too many ginger kittens around for it to be a coincidence.'

Maggie: 'She talked about you a lot. Always had something nice to say about you. I think she had a bit of a crush on you to tell the truth.'

'I'm flattered,' Winkle said. 'But is there nothing else? Anything you can think of, no matter how trivial or unimportant it seems?'

Maggie: 'She said business was a bit slower than usual.'

Annie: 'That was before she met that Nancy.'

Winkle started upright, his senses suddenly alert. 'Nancy?' he said, visions of his encounter in the alley slamming back into the forefront of his mind. 'Did she give you a last name?'

Annie: 'No. Just said she met someone called Nancy who

was putting some work her way. Couple of month's back this was. Said it was a different sort of punter. No pokey-pokey. Sounded weird to me.'

'And that was all she said?'

Annie: 'Said it was sort of a secret. I thought she was pulling my leg.'

Winkle stood up. 'Ladies, it's been a pleasure, as always.'

Maggie: You going, luv?'

'Yes, but you've been most helpful.'

Sandy: 'Have we?'

'Yes, I think so anyway.'

Julie: 'You'll let us know if you get the bugger, won't you?'

'You will be the first to know, I promise.'

As Winkle made his way to the door, Annie called out: 'You take care, luv. There's some real nasty bastards out there.'

Truer words were never spoken Winkle thought.

14

Five pubs. Five pints. Five shorts. After that, Winkle stopped counting. He had spent the day chasing down leads. That's what he called it anyway. In reality he had slogged around the streets until he was footsore and heartsick. Nobody knew anything. Or, if they did, they weren't talking. His old contacts were sympathetic but unhelpful. None of them had heard of anyone called Nancy. With a sinking sense of finality, Winkle realised that this private eye nonsense was okay on the telly but in reality you needed an organisation behind you. Resources that were now and forever beyond his reach.

If the drink didn't bring oblivion it at least blurred the edges of reality enough to make it bearable. By the time he reached the King's Head Winkle was as blurred as a newt, but he managed to order another pint and a whiskey chaser with a minimum of swaying and a modicum of slurring.

The pub was busy, a dozen or so young women decked out in sequins, short skirts, L plates and feather boas on a hen night and several leery lads hoping for a pre-nuptial fumble were crowding out the bar and raising the decibel level with inebriated screeches that passed for laughter, but he managed to find a seat at a battle-scarred table that may have wobbled or maybe that was just him. A wide screen TV was playing the local news, the newscaster's voice barely discernible above the hen party revellers.

'The police have today issued a statement advising the public to be extra vigilant following the second murder in as many days. The victims have not yet been named but are believed to be sex workers living in and around the area of

the city known as The Triangle.'

Winkle turned his face away from the screen. It's true what they say, he thought, nothing worth watching on TV these days. A voice filtered through his layers of alcohol. A voice from among the crowd at the bar. A voice he knew.

'Here,' it said, 'here's a good one. What's the difference between a hooker and an onion?'

No-one seemed to know and the voice was happy to provide the answer. 'You can cut a hooker without crying!'

Everyone seemed to find that hilarious. Everyone except Winkle.

I know that voice. *I know that voice.* And then it hit him. The memories came flooding back with such force he felt like they would drown him.

*

Rufus was black but that was the least of his problems. He was old too, but that was a cross everyone had to bear if they lived long enough. The fact that he smelt and was filthy he regarded as a personal hygiene statement that people could accept or not, the choice was theirs. The rheumatism was a curse, but with enough rum inside him he could almost forget that. Oh, yes, Rufus was also an alcoholic. He didn't regard it as a problem, more a fact of life.

Winkle had known Rufus for years. They'd put the world to rights too many times to count. He hadn't seen him for a while and he wasn't looking for him now.

The streets had been cold, hard and pointless on this particular night. It was a nothing case going nowhere. A flasher had been spotted lurking in the bushes on the common, the complainant too pissed to offer any useful information. Her only real complaint seemed to be that she didn't get a long enough look at the miscreant's appendage before he ran off. Winkle decided to call it a day, then he saw something that changed his mind.

There were three of them. Disaffected youths. For that read violent anti-social deviants. Anything illegal and excessive was their drug of choice and easy meat their preferred target. Rufus fell neatly into that category. Too old and slow to run, too weak to fight. Even from a distance it was easy to make out Rufus's shambling bulk. The three yobs had him surrounded. It was a familiar routine. First the verbal. Mock pleasantries. Lend us a fiver. Got a fag? Any booze? Then the physical. The shoves. The punches. The kicks. Like jackals they would go in for the kill. Winkle knew their names, knew their record but wasn't in the mood for the niceties of the law. That was their bad luck. He quickened his pace and when he was within easy calling distance said:

'I think you three geniuses have taken a wrong turn. The MENSA Meeting's at the Town Hall.'

Yob One, known to all and sundry as SV or String Vest if you were being formal because he always wore said garment, turned to look at Winkle. Yob Two, Trevor "Dickie" Dickson, had Rufus's arm twisted painfully behind his back. Yob Three, Bernie Edison, no relation, and, if he had been, he would definitely have been the black sheep of the family, stood off to one side shifting nervously from foot to foot.

Winkle continued strolling towards them until he was close enough to smell the glue on their breath.

'Still, never mind,' Winkle continued. 'You know what they say. If you're ever lost, you can always ask a policeman.'

'You ain't no fuckin' policeman.' SV said.

'Am I not?'

'No, you fuckin' ain't.'

'That's good, because if I was I might get into trouble for doing this.'

The blow came without warning or preamble. A hard, open-handed slap to the face that spun SV's head to one side so violently that Rufus would swear afterwards that he heard the bones in the boy's neck snap. Although not that lethal, the force of the blow was enough to knock the youth to the ground. Enraged by this outrageous treatment of his friend, Dickie Dickson let go of Rufus's arm and let out a strangled war cry before launching himself straight at Winkle.

The second blow was delivered with the same economy and effectiveness as the first. A straight right to the face, the heel of his hand making contact with his opponent's nose. There was a sharp crack and a spray of red that stopped Dickie in his tracks. 'Never punch someone with a closed fist if you can help it,' Winkle told him. 'You're liable to break your knuckles.' Dickie held his hands up to his face to catch the deluge of blood.

'You broked by dose!' he said.

Winkle nodded. 'And now I'm going to break your balls,'

he said. He took half a step back, shifted his weight onto his leading leg, pivoted and swing his size twelve with a skill that spoke of a rugby man. Dickie howled in a pitch that would have shattered crystal as the copper's toe-cap connected with its target and collapsed onto his already fallen comrade. Bernie Edison, no genius here, took a step sideways, his hand reaching into his pocket, fumbling with nervous fingers. Winkle watched him with barely concealed disinterest.

'Whatever you've got there,' he said, 'it had better have the stopping power of a bloody bazooka or else I'm going to take it off you and shove it up your arse. Sideways.'

Bernie thought about it and all movement ceased.

'Good decision,' Winkle told him. 'Now, do your good deed for the day and clean up this mess.' He gestured to the two groaning bodies on the ground. Bernie edged forward and with much groaning and moaning, dragged his companions to their feet. Their epithets faded on the night air as they staggered away. Rufus let out a wheezing cackle and slapped both rheumatic knees in delight.

'Mista Winkle, Sir,' he said. 'You sure is a sight for sore eyes.' Rufus always called Winkle "Sir". Since his arrival in England in 1957 Rufus prided himself that he had become an expert on the English character. He'd seen the good and the bad. And then there was Winkle. He didn't fall into any easily identifiable category of class, profession or belief. He was simply a friend and that fact alone merited the respect Rufus habitually showed.

'You need to start moving in better circles, Rufus,' Winkle said. *'Come on, I'll walk you home. St. James' Palace is it?'*

Rufus nodded. St. James' Hostel was a regular resting place when his old bones felt too fragile for life on the streets, something that was happening more and more often these days.

'Come on then,' said Winkle. 'Before they give the Honeymoon Suite away.'

*

That had been nearly twenty years ago, but it all came flooding back. It was that voice that brought all the sad, painful memories back to the surface. That same raddled face now sporting a scruffy beard. String Vest, alive and kicking and still picking on those that can't fight back. Picking on Peggy.

'You can cut a hooker without crying!'

Winkled levered himself to his feet. Swayed left, then right, found a tipping point somewhere in the middle and hurled his considerable bulk forward like a kamikaze full-back heading over the line. His fist took SV on the side of the head, sending him reeling. Winkle's momentum slammed him into the bar. He turned and tried to speak, but the words became tangled in his throat and all he could muster was an inarticulate roar. Common sense told him to run, his legs told him to forget it. His knees were already buckling when the first retaliatory punch landed. Winkle never knew how many there were. Didn't even feel the punches or the kicks after the first dozen or so. By the time the barman pulled them off, Winkle was unconscious.

'Jesus!' the barman muttered looking down at the dishevelled mess on the beer soaked floor. 'Drag him outside,' he said. 'If he snuffs it, I don't want him found in here.'

15

In the end, Winkle hadn't been hard to find. Dolly had started in The Bull where she had first met him. The barman had been suspicious at first, but had eventually given her Winkle's name and the fact that he was a copper. Did he know where Winkle lived? No, he didn't, but he did give her a list of the most likely pubs that Winkle frequented.

It was the third one Dolly tried when she found him. Not so much in the pub itself but close by. In the gutter. Beaten and bloody and barely conscious. Dolly dialled 999. She stayed by Winkle's side until the sirens could be heard then quickly faded into the shadows. No point in hanging around, she reasoned. Her message could not be delivered and maybe now he was going to hospital they might possibly be able to do something to help him. Possibly. But what could have led him to that lonely gutter? Dolly had no idea but it made her heart sink with the possibilities.

16

'Winkle?'

'Pardon?'

Ida waved her hand dismissively. 'Roy Pilkington. It's what everyone calls him. Are you sure it's him?'

Dolly nodded and sipped her tea. They were sitting in the kitchen of the Diamond Sauna and Massage Parlour, Ida's pride and joy for the last twenty years or more. A safe haven for street girls and a welcome retreat for gentlemen of all persuasions seeking comfort and relaxation. 'It's what the barman called him,' Dolly said.

'Well, they'd know,' Ida muttered.

'And he had a warrant card in his pocket, so, yes, it's definitely him.'

'And you're sure he's heading for the knackers yard?'

'My instincts are never wrong.' She paused. 'Not often anyway. But not this time, I swear.'

'Poor bugger.' Ida paused, her eyes drifting to images of years past. 'He's one of the good guys is Winkle. Never judged. Always on the side of the girls if one on their pimps got a bit handy. Used to carry some of my business cards to hand out to any new arrivals. Said if they were ever in trouble or needed a hand to come see me. Then he'd buy 'em a cuppa and a bag of chips, the daft sod. The number of times …' she stopped, her attention snapping back to the here and now. 'Enough of sodding memory lane. What are we going to do?'

Dolly shrugged. 'What can we do?'

'And he had a soft spot for Peggy you say?'

'One of her regulars. She had a bit of a thing for him too,

so it seems.'
  'Then we have to do something.'
  'He's not got much time, Ida.'
  'Then we'd better get a move on hadn't we?'

17

If I was a woman, Winkle thought, I'd like to be Ida Bone. When Winkle had first met Ida, she was in her late teens or early twenties, he'd never asked her age and she hadn't told him. She was all leather mini-skirts and fishnet stockings in those days, a mound of flaming red hair falling way past her shoulders. He met her on the corner of Spring Road, a well-known shop window for hookers. She had marched right up to him, bold as brass. Her opening gambit was: 'You must be Winkle. I've heard you're not a complete bastard.' That was Ida. Fearless and feisty through and through. It had been the start of a beautiful friendship. Now, thirty years later, Ida still prowled her patch like a lioness stalking game, but she no longer earned her living on the streets. Nowadays she ran Diamond Sauna and Massage and played mother hen to all the street girls, especially the young ones. Diamond gave them a safe place to go to when they got scared. Somewhere to have a cup of tea and a chat. Somewhere that even the most vicious pimp or disgruntled punter knew better then to intrude lest they feel the full wrath of an enraged Ida Bone. Winkle had witnessed Ida off the leash only once and it had chilled him to his marrow. A drunken middleweight called Terry Mossop had too much of a skinful and took it out on a seventeen year old waif called Sally Dean. Bruised, bloody and half naked, Sally had managed to run as far as Diamond before Mossop caught up with her. Winkle had been the first on the scene. The screams could be heard two streets away and Winkle feared the worst. He was half right. Mossop could have been a contender, but that night Ida had reduced him to a snivelling child crying for his mummy. All Winkle could do was stand back in awe. No charges were pressed and, when Mossop's opponents started calling him "Cry Baby Mossop" he gave up pugilism for a milk round in Stevenage.

None of which explained why Ida appeared at his hospital bedside that morning. She took one look at him and said: 'Blimey, what happened to your face? It looks like a kicked football.'

'The Botox wore off,' Winkle grunted. 'What are you doing here? How did you know I was even in hospital?'

Ida pulled up a chair. 'Thanks, I will have a seat, ta ever so.' She sat down and adjusted the hem of her skirt modestly, possibly, Winkle thought, for the first time in her life.

'I keep my eyes and ears open. Nothing much gets past me.' She paused. 'I'm sorry about Peggy.'

Winkle nodded and wished he hadn't. Ida glanced around the ward. Two of the other three beds were occupied, one by a skeleton in striped pyjamas who was catching flies and doing an impression of the two-thirty from Charing Cross, and the other by a blue rinse matriarch with half-moon glasses and a crossword puzzle. Neither seemed to be taking any notice of them, but Ida got up and pulled the pale green curtains around the bed anyway.

'Unless you're planning on giving me a bed bath, I don't know what you're doing that for.' Winkle said.

'I've got something to tell you. Something private.'

'They're not bloody soundproof you know.'

Ida sat on the hard plastic chair by Winkle's bed and leaned forward, speaking softly.

'I'm worried about you Winkle. I know what you're like.' She pointed to his face. 'This is what happens when you stick your nose in where it's not wanted. It could be so much worse if you've got some sort of vigilante aspirations.'

'That's a big word. You got a licence for language like that?'

'I'm serious Wink. For once in your life, do as you're told and let the police handle it.'

'I might. If I had anything to lose.'

'Peggy wouldn't want you to get hurt.'

'I don't mean Peggy.'

Winkle took a deep breath and told her. For the first time he used the dreaded C word in relation to himself. It felt awful. It felt cathartic. It felt right. Ida reached out and held his hand.

'Bloody hell, Wink, I am so sorry.'

Winkle sniffed. Wink, he thought. Ida was the only one who called him that. A shortened form of a nickname that was already shortened. If it gets any shorter, I'll disappear altogether, he thought. 'Sod that,' he said. 'Look in that locker will you and see if you can find my clothes.'

'You can't go. They want to keep you in for another twenty-four hours to see if that kick in the head knocked loose what few brain cells you still have left.'

'How do you know?'

'I asked.'

'They wouldn't even tell me that!'

'You don't have my charm. I said I was your sister.'

'I still need my clobber. I've got to feed the cat.'

'I can get you a bedpan if you like.'

'I mean the Chairman.'

'The Chairman? Peggy's cat? Have you got him?'

'Oh, yea. He sort of attached himself to me.'

'Can't he catch his own dinner for a couple of days?'

'He's not that sort of cat. He likes to be waited on.'

'Like his owner.'

'And he'll crap all over the place if I don't get back to him soon.'

'All right, but you stay put. I'll do it.'

'You?'

'Yea, me. I like cats. Or don't you trust me?'

Winkle sighed. 'Don't have much choice, do I?'

'Not a lot.'

'The keys are in my jacket pocket. Be careful though, he bites.'

Ida grinned. 'So he is just like his owner.'

18

The Priest was not a very holy man.

He consoled himself with that thought.

After the incident at the Church the Priest came to see Mother.

He came to pray.

He stayed for so much more.

A holy man would not have condoned his Mother's actions.

A holy man would not have looked on with such obvious interest as she stripped him.

A holy man would not have given his blessing as she beat him raw with his father's belt.

And then, when he had been sent to his room with just a Bible for company, a holy man would not have slipped between his Mother's sheets the better to consummate their prayers.

*

The undertakers lowered the casket into the ground and discretely withdrew, leaving him alone with the Priest. He stood at the edge of the grave and stared down at her final resting place. The Priest placed a hand upon his shoulder. 'She was a fine woman,' he said. 'If there is anything I can do, you just have to ask.' There was a tremor in the Priest's voice, a fever in his eyes. *He wants to take Mother's place.* The violence excited him that was obvious and now he wanted to experience it for himself. *The Priest is an Abomination.*

*

On his way back from the cemetery he stopped at a restaurant called "Steak 'n' Stuff". It was still early, the evening rush still some hours away. A waitress said 'Hi, I'm Cindy and I'll be your server today' and showed him to a table, placing a menu in front of him. He didn't need it.

'Steak,' he said.' The biggest one you have. And rare. As rare as possible. I like it rare.'

Cindy gave him a nervous smile. 'All the trimmings?' she said.

'Yes, I want everything.'

Mother had never let him eat meat. 'The juices will inflame your senses,' she said. By "juices" she meant the blood. As he waited for Cindy to bring his order he felt a churning, rushing sensation sweep through him. Like waves crashing on the shore they made him sweat, they gave him the chills. They sounded like laughter. A voice inside his head, a voice he had known was there for years but had never been able to fully break through Mother's barrier of pious pain whispered in his ear. *'Free,'* it said. *'We are free!'*

On the way home he threw up. His stomach was roiling from the unaccustomed meat. He bent over someone's wall and vomited in their flower bed. The scent of the regurgitated animal flesh made his eyes stream. Someone in the house banged on the window and shouted. He ignored them and walked on. He felt giddy, light-headed.

Everything had changed.

Nothing had changed.

Mother was gone.

He was his own man.

He was free to make his own decisions.

Free to follow his destiny.

His stomach gurgled but this time it was with excitement.

What would he do now?

*

He found the key in an old coffee tin in the kitchen cupboard. It was the one room in the house he had never been allowed into, at the back of the house overlooking the garden. He always hoped he might be allowed to move into this room. He liked looking at the garden, seeing things grow, so full of life and hope. But Mother always said no. It was always "your father's room". That's what Mother had said. Even after his father died, that room was always off limits. He had always wanted to know what was inside. Curiosity burned like a fever inside him. Now he would know.

His hand was shaking as he turned the key in the lock. At first sight it was just a room. A music room. There were guitars, amps, records, a hi-fi and clothes. Stage costumes by the look of them. Blood red silk shirts and leather jackets and trousers. His father's clothes. His father had been a musician, that much he knew, but Mother had never played any of his music, had allowed no music at all in fact save for some orchestral church organ pieces. The one item that really caught his eye though, sat on a small pedestal, resting on a purple silk cloth like an icon or religious relic of great importance. A human skull. Yellowed and malicious, it seemed to stare at him. At him and through him. Deep inside where the dark thoughts lived. A prop, he told himself. Something his father would have used on stage.

I am real.

The words popped into his head so suddenly he looked around to see who was standing behind him. No-one. He

turned back and the rigid jaw bones gaped at him in such a way that he could almost hear the laughter emanating from the bleached mouth.
Let me help you.
'No,' he muttered. 'This is not happening.'
I know what you want.
'I don't want anything.' This is crazy. I'm talking to myself. I'm going mad. But he knew he wasn't.
You want revenge on those that have wronged you
He nodded, afraid to admit it out loud. The Priest, that slut who had seduced him and made him kill his own mother, at least that's how it felt to him at the time, pretty much everyone he went to school with who had teased and bullied him ... the list was endless, wasn't it? Too many. It's impossible, isn't it?
I can make it happen. If you help me to gain my revenge in return.
 'Can you really do that?'
Trust me. I helped your father. I can help you.
Flustered, he took one of the albums out of its garish sleeve and placed it on the turntable. He sat cross-legged on the floor and listened to the voice coming from the speakers his back deliberately to the object on the pedestal. His father's voice. He picked up the album sleeve and read the lyrics. Mouthed along with his father's voice. As the record ended, he smiled. It all made so much sense now. This is what Mother had been hiding from him all these years. This is what she had tried to beat out of him. But Mother was gone now. So was his father and that was a shame. He would have had so much to teach him. Mother was right about one thing. He **was** like his father. Like him, he knew what he must do. He must follow his destiny. With that realisation

came release and he threw back his head and laughed out loud.
Do we have a deal?
He wanted to say "yes", wanted it so badly he felt faint with excitement at the very thought. But he had to be sure.

19

'Take your clothes off,' she told him. The money was safely tucked away, no need to drag this out. It was late and she was tired.

Brenda looked at him closely. He was nice looking. About her own age she reckoned. He had a nice body she thought. Bit skinny maybe, but nice apart from that. By now he was naked. There wasn't much going on between his legs but that wasn't unusual at this stage. Once the treatment started they usually perked up a bit. Nothing about his face or his body seemed familiar.

'It's the full works you want, don't you? I mean, that's what you paid for.'

He nodded. 'Oh, yes. The full works would be very nice.'

Brenda faked a cough to suppress a smile. 'All right then,' she said. 'Let's get you all nice and uncomfortable shall we?'

She started on his buttocks. The first stroke made a soft whapping sound.

'Harder,' he said.

Brenda obliged.

'Harder.'

Brenda swung with more force.

'Harder.'

By the end of the session she was sweating and her arm and shoulder ached. None of the others had been this much work. She was panting as she unbuckled him. His back, legs and buttocks were red raw, she could feel the heat coming from him.

As he faced her she saw that there was still no activity

between his legs. Pity, she thought, I'd have liked to see that one angry.

She turned away from him, giving him some privacy as he dressed. It was a funny thing but she always felt more embarrassed at this bit than all the rest. She sensed movement behind her. Something smooth slid around her neck. She started to say something but her breath was choked off. Panicked now, she tried to scream but no sound came out. She tried to struggle but his grip was too strong. She clawed at the leather band around her throat, reached behind her, scratching and slapping but the angle was wrong and she encountered nothing but sweat drenched flesh.

As he pulled tighter she felt something hard press into her buttocks. Her last conscious thought was that at least he'd managed to get it up at last.

*

It wasn't the same. Mother's beatings had been things of terrible beauty and agonised love. This was just a business transaction. 'I'll beat the devil out of you.' That's what Mother had always said. The skull had promised him revenge and salvation of a sort but it had scared him. He had to know if this was his destiny. Mother had always been right, hadn't she? It had been his own weakness and the evil ways of that slut Trixie that had caused Mother's death, but to do the things that the skull kept whispering into his brain? Surely that was wrong. Mother would know, but Mother wasn't here anymore. But someone else, someone who could beat the devil out of him, that would be just as good. Wouldn't it? He thought it might save him, but it hadn't. If anything, it had damned him forever. The rage that had come over him at her abject failure. The savage joy when her blood started to flow. God, that felt good. To cut, to see red rivers running down her pale flesh, the smell, the coppery taste on his tongue! To bring this sort of retribution on all those who had failed him in some way over the years. That was real power, that was his destiny.

'I'm yours,' he whispered.

And somewhere deep in his mind he heard the laughter of dead bones.

20

'I ought to report you to the RSPCA.' Ida was waiting for him the next day when the NHS released him without time off for good behaviour. Winkle hunched himself deeper into his overcoat and carried on walking. Ida fell into step beside him.

'There wasn't a tin of cat food in the entire place. Just some crumbly old biscuits.'

'I've not had chance to get to the shops lately,' Winkle grumbled.

'It's a wonder the poor thing didn't starve to death.'

Winkle snorted. 'Have you seen the size of him? He could hibernate longer than a grizzly bear the amount of blubber he's got on him.'

Ida continued unabashed. 'Anyway, he's all right now. I bought him some tuna.'

'You'll spoil him.'

'Someone's got to.' She linked her arm in his. 'Come on, the car's over here. You're staying with me until you properly recuperate. No arguing. It's settled'

Winkle knew better than to put up a fight and gave in as gracefully as he knew how.

*

A bright pink motorbike and sidecar was parked outside Ida's house. When Winkle saw it he gave a low whistle. 'Bloody hell, what's that?'

'That is the Pink Lady. It belongs to Trixie. She's my lodger.'
'You've got a lodger?'
'Yes, but don't worry, there's plenty of room. You won't

have to share a room with her or anything.'

Winkle grunted and heaved himself out of the car. He crossed to the motorbike and inspected it.

'It's a BMW R 67 Motorcycle Combination!' he said, almost breathless with admiration. 'In good nick to. Except for the colour which is an affront to civilisation.' He stood up and stretched the kinks out of his back. 'Haven't seen one of these around for donkey's years.'

'It's a 1951 model apparently' Ida said. 'Trixie did it up herself.'

'Really?'

'Yes, really. She uses it for work. She's a mobile hairdresser. Now, if you've finished drooling, come on in and I'll introduce you.'

As Winkle crossed the threshold, a portly ginger bundle trundled down the hallway and rubbed around his legs. 'Traitor,' Winkle mumbled, but bent to fondle the Chairman's ears nonetheless. The Chairman purred loudly, then waddled off to curl up in an armchair. 'I see he's made himself at home,' Winkle said.

Ida nodded. 'Very intelligent creatures, cats. Come on, I'll make you a cuppa.'

In the kitchen, a young woman with pink hair, plaid mini skirt, ripped tee-shirt, and enough piercings to give an airport metal detector apoplexy was leaning against the sink drinking a cup of coffee.

'Winkle, meet Trixie,' Ida said. 'Trixie, this is Winkle.'

Trixie pushed herself away from the sink and held out her hand. Winkle took it. Her hand was smooth and dry, her grip firm and friendly. A good handshake, he thought. 'Hi,' she said, smiling. 'Ida told me about what happened.' The smile dimmed. 'Really not cool. So sorry.'

Winkle shrugged. Whether she was talking about his beating or Peggy's death, he couldn't tell, but decided to ignore both topics. 'I was admiring your bike,' he said. Her smile returned full force. 'Yea, she's pretty special,' she said. 'She gets me where I want to go anyway.'

'Ida said you're a hairdresser.'

'Yea.' She appraised Winkle with a professional eye. 'I'll give you a trim if you want.'

Winkle ran his hand over his dome's sparse covering. 'You'll have to find some first,' he said.

'No probs. I do manscaping as well.'

Winkle frowned. 'What the hell's manscaping?'

Ida nudged his arm. 'I'll tell you later. When you're old enough.' She turned to Trixie.

'Don't you have an appointment at half past?'

'On my way.' Trixie dumped the remains of her coffee in the sink and rinsed the cup. 'See you later,' she said, and was gone. As Ida busied herself making tea, Winkle said: 'What's her story?'

'What makes you think she's got a story?'

'Everyone has a story.'

Ida placed two cups of tea on the table and they sat facing each other. 'Not very unusual,' she said. 'Her mother was an alcoholic, her father was in the wind. She put up with a succession of "Uncles" sticking their hand up her nightie until she was sixteen, then she left home. Teamed up with a punk tribute band. She's got a good voice as it happens. That went okay until their manager ran off with all their money. The band split up and she ended up stripping somewhere north of Hull.'

'Chilly work.'

'You're not kidding. She came back for her mum's funeral

and decided to stay. She was working the streets when I met her. I could see she wanted better so ...'

'You took her under your wing. Bit of a soft touch, are you?'

'Better than a crusty old cynic.' Ida smiled. 'She's a good kid. I gave her a place to stay and helped her train as a hairdresser. I've not regretted it. Seems I'm a good judge of character after all.'

They drank their tea in silence for a while, then Ida said: 'Come on, I'll show you your room.'

21

Trixie felt bony fingers on her inner thigh, inching their way higher like Incey Wincey spider climbing up the spout. She clamped her legs together and the invading fingers stopped, imprisoned between her warm flesh. She bent lower. Mr Bradshaw looked up at her with feigned innocence in his rheumy eyes.

'Old bones are very brittle Mr. B,' she told him, squeezing her legs together as hard as she could. 'And these scissors are very sharp.' She snapped the blades together to emphasis the point. 'We wouldn't want any accidents to happen now would we?'

He gave her a wan smile. 'I was just reaching for my jelly babies,' he wavered.

'I've heard it called a lot of things,' she told him, 'but that's a new one even for me.' Trixie relaxed her thighs and the intruding fingers withdrew. She watched him raise his hand to his face and sniff appreciatively. She shook her head. There's life in these old dogs yet, she thought.

Trixie began to snip away at Malcolm Bradshaw's sparse locks when a movement caught her eye. His name was Adam Bell but everyone called him Tinkerbelle, Tink to his friends. It wasn't hard to see why. He wore the regulation light blue jacket and dark blue trousers with a catwalk flourish and dared anyone to say that his full, sooty lashes were anything but natural. Trixie watched him make his way through God's waiting room like a particularly cheesy game show host dispensing bonhomie and gumdrops, leaving dentured smiles in his wake.

'Usual today, Malcolm is it?' he asked as he homed in on

them. 'Or shall we go mad and do a Mohican? I think you'd suit a Mohican, don't you?'

'Enough of your cheek,' Malcolm told him. 'I'm just having a touch up if you please.'

'You should be so lucky!' Tinkerbelle hooted.

'Don't give him ideas,' Trixie told him. 'He has enough of his own.'

'You can never have too much of a good thing,' he said. 'And how's Madame Trixie today?' he asked.

Trixie grinned. 'Bearing up,' she said

'Still going in for the bin liner chic I see,' he said, running a practiced eye over her plaid mini skirt, ripped tee-shirt, Doc Martens and silver studded leather wrist bands.

'Good taste never goes out of fashion' she smiled.

'You tell him love,' Malcolm said.

'One of these days I'm going to get my pal Swan to run her tape measure over you,' Tinkerbelle said. 'She's a wizard on the Singer. Knocks up all her own clothes. She'll have you kitted out like a Princess in no time.'

'I'd like that,' Trixie said. 'Let me check when I'm free. How about when Hell freezes over?'

Malcolm chuckled and sucked his teeth back into position.

'You can mock, but one day you'll come begging for a makeover, you mark my words.' Tink gave her a broad wink and turned to go. 'Have a good one sweetheart,' he told her as he moved off to spread more cheer and delight to the sick and needy. Trixie watched him go with a smile on her face. She liked Tink. Despite their obvious differences they had one thing in common: neither one of them would bow to public opinion. They were individuals first and foremost and anyone who didn't like it could sling their hook.

Malcolm beckoned Trixie closer. As Trixie leaned in, batting away waving digits that were too close to her breasts for comfort, he said: 'He's a bum boy.'

Trixie giggled. 'I know that, Malcolm.'

'Just thought I'd tell you in case you ever shake his hand. If you do, be sure to wash in carbolic after. You never know where his hands have been.'

'You shouldn't say things like that Macolm. It's not PC.'

'What's that? Pissy, you say? I should think he probably is. And the rest. Makes them loose, you know. Well, hardly surprising is it, shoving things where things have no right being shoved.'

Trixie snorted a laugh into the back of her hand and tried to pretend it was a sneeze. Deaf as a post with an opinion on anything and everything, Malcolm Bradshaw was not the sort to go quietly. I want to be like him when I get old, Trixie thought.

*

Dolly waved to Trixie as she passed. Tink was busy reducing old ladies to giggling schoolgirls, no-one was having a funny turn and lunch was still over an hour away. More than enough time for a quick visit she told herself.

The residents of Denby Lodge all had their own apartments. Privacy if they wanted it, but enough company and communal activities to stop them feeling lonely. Sir Francis generally kept himself to himself. Not that he was stand-offish and everyone liked him, but he was a private person. Comes with the territory, Dolly thought.

Dolly tapped discretely on his door. She heard him call: 'Come in,' and she entered. Sir Francis's apartment was small, neat and tidy, almost Spartan. He sat in a comfortable armchair, his mane of thick silver hair swept back from a high forehead, his eyes were faded blue and his smile quick and warming. He smiled at her now and she felt her blood race as she returned his greeting. It had been Sir Francis who had found her when she was at her lowest ebb and turned her life around, given her a unique purpose and for that she was eternally grateful. It hurt her now to look into those pale blue eyes and see a sort of detached vacant stare. He was looking straight at her but she knew his mind was elsewhere, lost in the corridors of time, so much time, the weight of memories must be crushing.

Dementia

Alzheimers

Call it what you will, it was the cruellest blow, the most despicable burden to bear to leave the body intact but to deprive someone of everything that made them themselves. There was no cure. For most people anyway, but Sir Francis was not most people.

Dolly perched on the edge of the sofa and took his hand in hers. 'How are you today, Sir Francis?' she asked.

He smiled and nodded and Dolly felt her heart break just a fraction. 'Time for a little aperitif before lunch?' she said. There was a spark then, just a flicker, but enough to let her know that he was still in there.

Sir Francis chuckled, a sound like crystal waters over shining pebbles. 'You know how to tempt me,' he said.

Dolly took a small manicure case out of her pocket and opened it up. Inside lay a small, razor sharp scalpel, a syringe and a small vial of dark liquid. 'Draught or bottled?' she asked archly.

'You know I prefer it straight from the cask,' he chuckled.

Dolly nodded and rolled up her sleeve.

*

Afterwards, Sir Francis leant back in his chair and sighed. His face was suffused with colour and his gaze was focused and in the here and now.

'It's getting worse isn't it?' he said.

'It's manageable,' Dolly told him.

'Thanks to you my dear. Our brethren are forever grateful to you and all the other Nancy's. Without your ministrations we simply would not be able to survive.'

Dolly felt herself turn pink. Flustered as she always was by compliments. 'Have you been watching the news?' she asked.

Sir Francis nodded. 'You mean these "Slasher" killings? That's what the press have dubbed him is it not? The Slasher. Such a dearth of imagination. But still, most distressing. If this continues it could bring unwanted attention. Such things have happened before but not for many, many years. We may have no choice but to take direct action to resolve the situation. It's at times like this that I regret not having the services of the redoubtable Chief Inspector Abberline and Constable Colverson to act as our intermediaries.'

'I may have a solution to that particular problem,' Dolly said, and began to tell him about her encounter with Winkle. After she had finished Sir Francis gazed at her over steepled fingers. Lost in thought.

'And both victims were our sister's in blood?' he asked.

'Yes. And Mr. Pilkington was very close to Peggy, in a strictly civilian capacity of course.'

'Of course, of course. But that would mean that he would have every incentive to join our cause.'

'But will there be time? He is dying after all.'

Sir Francis waved away her objection. 'A not insurmountable problem.'

'But he knows nothing of our existence, our history, our culture. He will be difficult to convince. I've spoken to Ida about him and I got the distinct impression he could be quite stubborn.'

'Then he must be educated in our ways'

'But how?'

Sir Francis smiled. 'I think I have just the thing.'

22

The Chairman had adopted the most comfortable armchair in the way that cat's do and, apart from latrine duty in Ida's flower beds, seemed content to stay close to home.

Winkle scratched him behind the ears and he purred loudly. Winkle wandered into the kitchen and the cat dutifully followed him, waiting patiently as Winkle spooned cat food into a bowl.

Winkle watched him eat, then waddle back to his armchair where he curled up once more. Inside a minute he was sound asleep, snoring loudly. Winkle smiled and made his way upstairs. It's been a funny old day, he thought. Who'd have thought I'd end up sleeping in Ida Bone's spare bed? There was a time when it wouldn't have been the spare bed, he thought. But then, maybe I'm just kidding myself. Not that I'd have been tempted mind, but still, the offer would have been nice.

It wasn't until Winkle was safely ensconced in his best winceyette that he saw the envelope propped up on the bedside table. He picked it up. No stamp, his name hand written on the front. He didn't recognise the writing. What the heck is this? he thought. Only one way to find out.

Tucked up in bed, Winkle opened the envelope and slipped out several sheets of paper. It was getting late, but Winkle didn't feel sleepy. He began to read.

My Dear Mr. Pilkington

Allow me to introduce myself. My name is Francis Varney. Sir Francis Varney to be absolutely correct if such things

matter to you, but I confess that they mean less than nothing to me so do not feel compelled to acknowledge the fact in any way.

I have asked our mutual friend, Miss Ida Bone to pass this letter to you as I feel it may be to our mutual benefit if we met to discuss a common problem. The problem in question is the slaying of two women in a most horrific manner. One of whom was Peggy Li, a most charming individual who, I am led to believe, you harboured considerable affection for. My sincere condolences for your loss.

In the course of your police career, you may well have encountered many who were capable of committing such an atrocity, but let me assure you that in this instance the perpetrator does not fall into any category with which you may be familiar. How I know this will, hopefully, become clearer as you read the rest of this missive and clearer still if you agree to meet me in person, which, I hope you will for both our sakes.

Firstly, let me address the metaphorical elephant in the room. The mutual problem that faces us has a name. A name that has passed into common parlance as a phenomenon of mass entertainment and, all too often, a figure of fun.

Let me assure you that this phenomenon is all too real and the potential danger it represents should, under no circumstances be underestimated. The name of this phenomenon is:

Vampire

Your understanding of that term, shaped, as I am sure it has been, by centuries of literature and media interpretation is fundamentally different from my own.

I hope that the document you now hold in your hands will go some way to dispel the more preposterous illusions associated with that term. Allow me to begin, if you will, by explaining what a vampire is not.

A vampire is not a supernatural creature.

He, or she, is not a demon from some nether world.

Vampire's cannot turn themselves into bats, wolves or fog.

With very few exceptions, vampire's cannot hypnotise mortals into doing their will or drive them mad.

They do not crumble in sunlight.

They are not repelled by religious icons.

They do not sleep in coffins nor do they have razor sharp teeth.

They can, however, be killed by driving a stake through their heart or by decapitation or immolation by fire, but can the same not be said of any mortal being?

I could go on. The list of what a vampire is not is near inexhaustible. Rather, I would tell you what a vampire truly is.

The study of evolution tells us that Homo Sapiens evolved from Neanderthals, but, any scientist worthy of the name will confirm that there were many more species of humanity that evolved at the same time as Homo Sapiens were establishing themselves as the putative dominant species on this planet. Most of the divergent species were short lived and perished with little or no trace of them ever having existed. One of these minor species was the variant strain of humanity Homo Vampiris, or, simply, Vampires.

Possessing the majority of the Homo Sapiens' traits that enabled it to survive and prosper, the vampire's differed in one crucial aspect: their ability to sustain themselves on human blood. Not that this formed their diet exclusively. Vampires then, and now, can exist perfectly well on the sorts of food essential to the survival of any human being.

The ingesting of blood is, however, essential if a vampire is to survive without suffering severe mental and emotional decline. Please do not run away with the idea that a vampire is a ravening beast that stalks its prey and drains it dry in order to prolong its own unnatural existence. A vampire does, indeed, have a much prolonged lifespan and enjoys a more robust health than his "normal" counterpart, but this can be maintained with relatively small ingestions of blood at regular intervals. Indeed, rather than a murdering beast in human form, most vampires regard their peculiar dietary requirements as you would regard an allergy that dictated you refrain from consuming dairy or chocolate lest you suffer ill effects.

The majority of vampires therefore, wish only to live as normal a life as possible, keeping their predilections to themselves and are successful in doing so if they can obtain their modest blood requirements.

That is where I come in. It has been my pleasure and my calling to arrange for the discrete provision of willing donors to maintain the vampire population in health and secrecy. More of that later. To conclude this part of the correspondence I should, perhaps, touch on the subject of procreation. The idea that a vampire can take a human to the brink of death and revive them by giving them a transfusion of their own blood at the cost of turning them into a vampire is, in fact, quite possible, but has never been widely practiced. Vampires reproduce in the same way as any human, but it is by no means certain that such a union will produce a full-fledged natural born vampire. Many vampire offspring are completely human, hence the comparatively few vampires that exist today or have ever existed throughout history. A small percentage of vampire progeny, although human, do inherit the desire to drink human blood. This, regrettably, can lead to mental instability and the committing of heinous crimes that could, justifiably, be laid at the vampire's door, but whose numbers pale into insignificance when compared to the atrocities committed by fully-fledged humans with no vampire heritage.

I hope that this letter has, in some way, planted a seed of curiosity and persuaded you that a face to face meeting between us may be of some use if only to satisfy your idle curiosity as to the subject matter I have outlined. Miss Ida Bone would be only too pleased to arrange such a meeting at a time to suit your convenience.

Yours most sincerely
Sir Francis Varney

Winkle tossed the letter to one side. It was a bloody fairy story, that's what it was. The ravings of a madman at best. And yet ... Strip away the fancy trappings and what do you have? A sect that drinks human blood because they think it gives them superhuman powers. Bonkers, but people have killed for less, much less. If just one of these nut jobs believes in all this, would it be enough to make him go on a killing spree? Oh, yes. Any faith Winkle may have had in human nature had evaporated years ago when, as a brand new bobby with his first pointy hat, he had witnessed his first murder victim. He had thrown up all over his nice shiny boots that day and knew that he had glimpsed the real face of evil hidden behind the mundane façade of everyday life. Of course it was possible. And Ida of all people was mixed up in this somehow. If this Sir Francis Varney knows something about the people who adopt this sort of lifestyle he needs talking to. Winkle had half a mind to go and drag Ida out of bed right now and demand an explanation, but the thought of what Ida might or might not be wearing as bed attire gave him pause. Better to sleep on it, he thought, and tackle it fresh in the morning.

23

Next morning Winkle waited until he heard the sound of Trixie's motorbike grumbling off into the distance. Then he marched downstairs and slapped the envelope onto the breakfast table.

'What the bloody hell's this all about?' he demanded.

Ida shot him an icy glare. 'I knew you'd react like this if I told you. That's why we thought it best if you heard it from the horse's mouth.'

'Horse's arse more like!'

'Sit down,' Ida instructed. 'I've kept your breakfast warm for you. Grumbling, Winkle did as he was told as Ida retrieved a plate of bacon and eggs from the oven and put fresh bread in the toaster.

'Have you fed the cat?' Winkle wanted to know.

'Yes, I've fed the cat and he was much more appreciative than some people I could mention.'

Winkle pointed an eggy fork at the envelope. 'You can't really expect me to take that load of bollocks seriously?' he said.

'Nor did I at first. Then I listened to what he had to say. Wink, I've seen proof.'

'Proof? What sort of proof?'

The toaster popped and Ida retrieved the toast and began buttering it. 'How long have we known each other, Winkle?'

'What's that got to do with the price of spuds?'

Ida ignored him and carried on regardless. 'You wouldn't be this miffed if you really thought it was a load of bollocks. You'd have just tossed it in the bin or written it off as a bit of a joke. I'm right aren't I?'

'The bit about people *thinking* they're vampires might have a grain of truth in it. Have you got any marmalade?'

Ida fetched the marmalade from the cupboard and plonked it down in front of him. 'If you think there's that much truth in it, then what's the harm in meeting him and hearing what he's got to say? It's not as if you've got any other clues is it?'

Winkle grumbled into his toast as the doorbell sounded. Ida left him chewing and ruminating as she went to answer the door. The sound of muffled voices sounded down the passage and, when the door opened again, Ida ushered another woman into the room.

Winkle looked up. 'Bloody hell, it's Paddington Bear!' he said.

24

'I'm Dolly, Mr. Pilkington. Pleased to meet you properly at last.'

'Dolly? I thought you said your name was Nancy?'

'No. I said I was Nancy. It's more like a job title or a rank.'

'Do what?'

'We call ourselves Nancy after Sir Francis's wife. She founded our order.'

'Your order? Don't tell me your bloody nuns as well!'

'No. Oh, dear, I'm not really explaining this very well.'

'Stop flustering her, Winkle,' Ida said. 'It's not an interrogation. Let her speak.'

Winkle nodded for Dolly to continue.

'When we first met, I'm so sorry if I gave you a fright. You see, I had mistaken you for one of us.' Winkle raised an eyebrow. 'I have a sort of ... sixth sense. An instinct if you like. I can tell who is one of the brethren and who isn't. But I sometimes get my signals mixed up when a person is suffering from a terminal condition.'

Winkle's mouth dropped open. 'How did you ...?' he began. 'I haven't even had my marching orders from the quacks yet!'

Dolly's face reddened. 'I am sorry if I spoke out of turn. I didn't realise ... Oh dear, I'm making rather a mess of this again aren't I?'

'Maybe you'd better just take me to this Sir Francis character.'

'Yes, yes, of course. Sir Francis is the head of our order. He will give you all the information you need.'

25

'How do your ...clients find you?' Winkle asked. They were on their way to Denby Lodge in Dolly's blue Smart car. It was her pride and joy but Winkle felt like a sardine in a can. Pointless though he thought this journey was there were several practical aspects of Dolly's story that intrigued him. 'I mean, you can't exactly stick an ad in the paper can you? And I don't believe you all roam the streets picking up half dead drunks in pubs who look like they could use a little O-Neg pick-me-up.'

'That's how I met you,' Dolly told him.

'There's an exception to every rule,' Winkle muttered. 'And I wasn't drunk.'

'Not that time, no. And these days we're more likely to do something on-line rather than an ad in the paper, but there are lots of other ways. It was much more difficult in the old days, of course. Then it used to be just word of mouth. News spread slowly and people were much more aware of the existence of vampires because there was more evidence of vampire activity. Now it's much more common knowledge passed on from generation to generation within the fraternity that these services are available. That's why the vampire population has grown considerably, but very few people know of their existence.'

'Cuts down on the number of angry villagers with pitchforks and flaming torches if nobody knows you exist I suppose.'

'Exactly. Nowadays we use massage parlours a lot. That's where Ida comes into the picture. She helps recruit new Nancy's and acts as a sort of information hub for any vampires who are new in town.'

'Does Ida go in for this blood sucking lark?'

'Oh, no. Strictly an admin role. It's a sort of tradition. What she does is vital but it might pose a sort of conflict of interest if she was Nancy as well.'

'And Trixie? Is she a Nancy?'

'No. Ida didn't want to bring her into the sisterhood. Said it wouldn't be right after all she's been through. And it's not just sex workers who become Nancy's. We've got all sorts now. Doctor's, lawyers ...'

'Indian Chiefs?'

'If they wanted, we don't discriminate, but also housewives, supermarket checkout girls, barmaids, nurses or care workers like me. It's the perfect cover for home visits. But we also use hotels, casino's, anywhere really. There's even talk of opening a vampire theme park.'

'You're kidding?'

Dolly smiled. 'About that last one, yes, but Sir Francis is negotiating for a casino in Las Vegas.'

'He must be worth a fortune.'

'He is. He owns Denby Lodge, but he never lets on. It was his family home when his wife was alive.'

'The original Nancy?'

'Yes.' A sad expression crossed Dolly's face. 'She was the love of his life. She accepted him for what he was, both as a man and as a vampire. He loved her so much it broke his heart when she died. He offered to turn her, to give them an eternity together, but she refused. She said she could serve the community better as a mortal. It was her idea to use volunteers to supply blood to vampires you see, so they wouldn't have to hunt to survive.'

Dolly pulled in to the car park at Denby Lodge.

'And all the other old codgers who live here, are they all ...'

'Vampires? Heaven's, no. Only Sir Francis. He really has worked wonders for the community. Everyone keeps an eye out for everyone else. They make sure that all the newbies know where and how to get their treatment.'

'Treatment? Is that what you call it?'

'What else would you call it? It's what they need to keep them healthy. Without it, God only knows what would happen. It doesn't bear thinking about.'

'I suppose not, but why do you do it?'

'Do what?' she said.

Winkle levered himself out of the car and began to follow her towards the large old manor house that now played host to senior citizens of all types. 'This blood sucking thing,' he said. 'I'm not saying I believe in vampires, but why cut yourself and let some nutter suck your blood? It's not just kinky, it's masochistic.'

Dolly sighed. 'It's not all one way, you know. And keep your voice down. Sir Francis is the only one who knows about you-know-what.'

'All right, but what do you mean, it's not all one way?'

'I don't know the scientific reason, but there's something in a ...' she lowered her voice to a whisper ' ...vampire's saliva. It acts as a sort of aphrodisiac.'

'You're joking!'

'Gospel. Why do you think so many get hooked on it? One suck is all it takes and you can't wait for more.'

'It's really that good?'

'You come like an express train over and over. Normal sex just can't compete.'

'Flamin' Nora!'

Dolly grinned and opened the large oak carved front door. 'Here we are,' she said. 'I'll take you to meet Sir Francis.'

*

Dolly ushered Winkle into Sir Francis's room like a flunky introducing a commoner to royalty. She took up a seat at a discrete distance as Sir Francis shook Winkle's hand with a dry and surprisingly firm grip for someone of his age. Now, they sat in armchairs facing each other as Sir Francis steepled his fingers and regarded Winkle steadily.

'So, Mr. Pilkington, what did you make of my letter?'

Winkle opened his mouth to speak but Sir Francis held up his hand to forestall him. 'Let me guess,' he said. 'Ballderdash and tommyrot. Utter nonsense, am I correct?'

'Pretty much.'

'Splendid. In your position I would have thought much the same. But can we assume that the information it contained can form the broad basis for our discussion today?'

Winkle nodded. 'Why not? I've got nothing else to go on.'

'Refreshing honesty, Mr. Pilkington. Now, what do you know of the Ottoman wars of the 16th century?'

It wasn't the question Winkle had been expecting. He pondered for a moment. 'Bugger all,' he finally said.

Sir Francis laughed a throaty chuckle. 'Excellent! Then you will not be able to contradict me!' He laughed once more. 'Before I begin I must apologise for my appalling manners. I haven't offered you any refreshments. Some tea perhaps? Or coffee if you prefer? Something stronger perhaps? I'm sure the sun is over the yardarm somewhere in the world?'

Winkle accepted "something stronger" and Dolly poured them both a generous measure of a rather fine brandy.

Sir Francis smacked his lips in appreciation. 'Now, where was I? Ah, yes, the Ottoman conflict of the 16th century. The Ottoman's were a fierce and acquisitive military force, determined to conquer all of Europe and bring it under their rule. In their attempt to subdue Hungary they met considerable resistance led, in no small part, by a man named Ferenc Nadasdy, known as the Black Knight and famed as a military tactician and a savage warrior in battle. His success in war was partly due to the fact that he was a natural born vampire.

'Ferenc Nadasdy, the Black Knight of Hungary was killed by decapitation in 1604. I know this to be true because I carried out his execution myself at the command of King Henry VIII of England.'

'You knew Henry VIII? Personally?' Winkle said, incredulously.

'I did indeed. I was one of his most trusted lieutenants.'

'You realise that would make you over four hundred years old?'

'Closer to seven hundred actually, but I think I'm wearing rather well, don't you?'

Winkle opened his mouth but found he had nothing to say so Sir Francis continued his narrative.

'Now, where was I? Oh, yes. Anxious to enter a treaty with Sultan Mehmed III of the Ottoman Empire in order to ensure England's trading interests, King Henry had agreed to extract this particularly irritating thorn from Ottoman flesh as a sign of good will that England would not put troops into the field to oppose the Ottoman interests and so that their conquest of Europe could continue unimpeded. In return, the Sultan promised not to interfere with English trading activities. But how to bring about this desired result? The answer, as it so often is, was love.'

'Love? Winkle asked.

'Quite so. What will men not do for love, Mr. Pilkington? It is, I find, the prime motivator in most matters. Ferenc Nadasdy may have been an unremitting sadist on the field of battle, but in his private life he was a devoted husband. In 1575, Ferenc Nadasdy had married Elizabeth Bathory, a mortal, but one possessed of a cruel nature that matched, and maybe even excelled her husband's sadism since he reserved his sadism for enemy soldiers whereas Elizabeth used her position to torture and kill her servants simply because it amused her. Their marriage was therefore a happy one founded on their excessive cruelty and ruthlessness with which they ruled the region of Hungary known as Transylvania.'

'Elizabeth Bathory?' Winkle said.

'Ah, so you have heard of her?'

'Countess Dracula? Who hasn't?'

Sir Francis frowned in confusion. 'You've lost me, I'm afraid, Mr. Pilkington.'

'Hammer Horror. Igrid Pitt. No?'

Dolly leaned forward. When she spoke it gave Winkle a start. He'd forgotten she was still there. There was something about Sir Francis's manner, his voice, the intensity of his gaze that seemed to blot out all other sensory input. Even if he is spouting gobbledegook, Winkle told himself.

'It was a film, Sir Francis,' Dolly said. 'One of a series of so-called horror movies that played rather fast and loose with the vampire legend.'

Sir Francis brightened. 'Of course, of course! Yes, but this Elizabeth Bathory was the basis from which all subsequent legends sprang and her ferocity and cruelty on the homefront more than equalled her husband's prowess on the battlefield I can assure you. Another libation, Mr. Pilkington? All this talking makes one rather thirsty I find.'

Winkle accepted and, when the drinks were poured Sir Francis took up his tale.

'A direct assault on the field of battle was unlikely to succeed and so I decided to attack the one chink in the Black Knight's armour: his love for his wife.

'Accompanied by the Sultan's representative who was to ensure that our mission was indeed successful, I travelled with a band of mercenaries led by the Scottish warrior Angus Rawshank to Castle Cjeste in Transylvania, hereditary home of the Bathory clan and where Elizabeth Bathory resided. The castle itself was much too imposing an edifice to storm and so we adopted a much more subtle plan. Elizabeth's actions had made her a hated and despised person in the surrounding villages and it was relatively easy to find people who were only too willing to provide us with information on the best way to infiltrate the castle unobserved.

'With most able-bodied men away at war, the castle guards were old men and boys and easily dealt with once we had made our entry. The servants, of course, were only too pleased to allow us access to their mistress and summarily disappeared into the night never to return. Elizabeth herself spat and clawed and reviled us with most unladylike language, but it had little effect on armoured, battle hardened mercenaries and her capture was acquitted with remarkable ease.

'I gave strict orders that she was not to be harmed in any way. I was after all an English gentleman and she a member of the fairer sex. I then sent a messenger to the battleground where Ferenc Nadasdy was camped. The message informed him that his wife had been taken prisoner and would be summarily executed if he did not present himself at Castle Cjeste within three days. He was to tell no-one and to come alone. Any hint that he disobeyed this instruction would result in his wife's instant demise.

'Love, Mr. Pilkington, is a tremendous motivator, and this cold blooded killer and military strategist obeyed these instructions to the letter despite their obvious intent to lead him into a trap. Perhaps it was arrogance on his part, who knows, but he did, indeed, come charging up to Castle Cjeste three days later, alone.'

Despite himself, Winkle found himself caught up in the narrative. He wetted his lips and asked: 'So what happened?'

'We had prepared for his arrival, naturally. Men had been secreted in the surrounding countryside and throughout the castle, but what is a trap without bait I hear you ask? A very reasonable question. In order to tempt our prey into the jaws of destruction, we pulled a large wagon into the forecourt of the castle, leaving the outer gates conveniently open. To one of the wagon's wheels we bound Elizabeth Bathory, naked and helpless, for her husband to see. An ungentlemanly action I admit, but Rawshank assured me that we needed something to "sweeten the pot" as it were and she was a strikingly attractive woman so it was not all bad I have to admit. Moreover, it had the desired effect. At the sight of his wife thus displayed, Ferenc Nadasdy lost any remnants of logic and strategy and rushed to her side, throwing caution to the wind. It was then that the trap was well and truly sprung.

'As he hacked at her bonds and wept bloody tears, Rawshank's men surrounded him in a ring of steel. That did not prevent him from launching an attack however, and he claimed the lives of three of Rawshank's men before Rawshank himself bludgeoned him into submission.

'Securely bound and conscious once more, I confronted him before carrying out the sentence I had been employed to administer.

'I am Sir Francis Varney, envoy of his majesty King Henry VIII of England. By his orders and by the command of Sultan Mehmed III of the Ottoman Empire you are hereby sentenced to death. Do you have any last words?'

The look in his eyes was of purest evil as he spat his epitaph through clenched teeth.

'You have defiled the one I love the most. I swear by all that is unholy that I will track you down and destroy those you hold most dear before ending your life so that you too can know the pain that I feel. I swear I will do this even if it takes an eternity and I have to fight free from the very depths of Hell to do so.'

Having said his piece, Rawshank handed me the claymore specially prepared for the occasion and I did my duty to King and country. The Sultan's envoy took Nadasdy's severed head back to his Sultan and King Henry had his agreement. I have no idea what happened to his head after that although rumours surface from time to time but without verification.

We left Castle Cjeste as it was and gave it no more thought. Elizabeth Bathory was surrendered to the care of the villagers that she has so abused and they were not the most gentle of jailers, but that was none of my business. On my return to England, the King showed his gratitude by drafting the Covenant of Blood. A most secret document, it essentially acknowledged the existence of, not just vampires, but any and all other unspecified entities not conforming to the accepted parameters of humanity and appointing myself as guardian and protector of the realm against any and all such threats.

The Covenant lasted for many centuries until the advent of scientific advancement in the twentieth century rendered it obsolete and it was relegated to the status of a piece of medieval folklore. For myself, it mattered little. My main task was done and the Nancy network was well established by that time and I was able to retire from the field. It seems I may have been premature in my assessment of the situation.

'I confess, I was lax in my duty. You see, rumours had reached me for many years that Ferenc Nadasdy was making good on his threat to exact vengeance from beyond the grave.

'Legend has it that the spirit of Ferenc Nadasdy still inhabited the skull and reached out to any who shared the vampire heritage, be they natural born vampires or simply humans who had the potential to become such. Under the skulls influence, they were incited to commit murderous atrocities in the skull's attempt to exact Ferenc's vengeance by proxy. According to legend, the skull eventually found its way into the hands of Grigori Rasputin. What the so-called Mad Monk did with it is open to debate, but even he, it seems, could not cope with its power and its whereabouts were unknown for many years. Eventually it surfaced in the possession of a German merchant seaman called Carl Feigenbaum who was alleged to have commited several murders under its influence. Fleeing from the authorities, Feigenbaum fled to England where the skull passed into the hands of a Polish barber named Klosowski who was living under the pseudonym George Chapman. The exact circumstances of this transfer are unknown, but what is certain is that Chapman was the most accommodating of all the skull's caretakers, allowing the spirit of Ferenc Nadasdy to possess him completely. That, Mr. Pilkington, brings us to the events of 1888.'

LONDON 1888

'Five murders!' Commissioner Warren's ire was expressed in his flushed features and a fine spray of spittle.

'Six,' replied Detective Chief Inspector Abberline, a more placid individual. 'If you count Martha Tabram. Seven if you count ...'

'Five murders!' Warren roared. 'Five that we can definitely attribute to the same perpetrator. The man who that damned Gazette glorifies with the name "Jack the Ripper". And no arrests. Why is that, Inspector?'

'The small matter of proof is somewhat of a hindrance,' Abberline replied blandly.

'Proof? Proof? Good God, man, you have suspects coming out of your ears.'

'But unfortunately, no proof.'

'You want proof? What about McKenna? He threatened to stab people did he not?'

'According to several unreliable witnesses, yes.'

'Then arrest him and be done with it.'

'On the night of at least one of the murders, Edward McKenna was sleeping in a common lodging house at 15 Brick Lane. Several other slightly more reliable witnesses can attest to that.'

'Kosminski then.'

'Aaron Kosminski is a pathetic wretch who resides periodically at the Mile End Old Town Workhouse for the Insane. He eats out of the gutter and refuses to wash. It is unlikely that even the most raddled of whores would let him anywhere near her and every description we have of the Ripper says that he is well dressed and elegant. Besides,

Kosminski had been released into the care of his brother at the time of the murder. We have spoken to the brother who informed us that he would have noticed if his brother had returned home covered in blood.'

Warren thumped his desk with his fist. 'Good God, man, show some initiative. Pick a suspect and arrest him so we can at least get the damned press off our backs.'

'Even if he isn't Jack the Ripper?'

'As long as there is a reasonable case to make, the headlines will read: " Jack the Ripper caught". Which is a damned sight better than what they are saying at the moment.'

'And if I do that and the murders still continue?'

'There's more than one killer in London, Abberline. As long as everyone thinks Jack the Ripper is in custody that's all that matters. The reputation of Scotland Yard will be restored and any subsequent murders can be blamed on some other low-life miscreant. This will be done, Abberline, you mark my words. If not by you, then I'll find someone else who will.'

*

Back at Whitechapel, the men went about their duties with a degree of urgency but little faith that it would produce the required result. The Whitechapel Killer was a seeming ghost. Coming and going at will, leaving behind a trail of devastation but little or nothing in the way of clues. The city was awash with panic and false leads, each one more preposterous than the last. Abberline found himself reluctantly considering Sir Charles Warren's suggestion that any arrest would be better than none, if only to quell the tumult that held the population in its grip. He rejected the notion after no more than a second's serious consideration. Justice would not be served that way and without justice his role and that of the entire Scotland Yard were worthless.

As he passed along the corridor towards his office Constable

Colverson approached carrying a buff folder in his hand.

'How did it go, sir?' he asked.

Abberline gave a wry smile. 'About as well as you might expect. What do you have there?'

'A statement, sir. Not about the Ripper. At least, I don't think it is.'

'But you think it might be?'

'I don't know. It's a bit ...unusual. I was going to show it to you when you had a moment, to get your opinion.'

'No time like the present, Colverson. Come into the office and I'll give it a look.'

*

Once in Abberline's office, Colverson explained about the threadbare cleric and Sergeant. Thicke's insistence that he was not right in the head and should be ignored.

'But you beg to differ, Colverson?' Abberline asked.

Colverson shrugged. 'I don't rightly know, sir. His tale seems unlikely enough, but his manner is sincere. It may be that he's just misinterpreting the facts.'

'Pass it over then, Colverson and let's see what we have.'

Colverson handed over the folder and Abberline began to read.

Statement of Father Peter Cheshire concerning events occurring at Sanguine House as dictated to Constable William Walter John Colverson on this day the 25th of November in the year 1888.

My name is Peter Cheshire. By profession, inclination and moral certainty, I am a man of God. I have heard it said that the surest proof of God's existence is the undeniable presence of evil in our society. For if the Devil exists in

these acts, can we deny that God too must be real? If that is so, then I have witnessed first-hand such evidence of evil in its purest form that can only have been the work of Satan himself as to render my faith in the Almighty unshakeable and incontestable by even the staunchest of unbelievers.

My parish is a poor one. The people destitute and, for the most part, good, but driven to sin by the grinding poverty of their lives and the callous indifference of their fellow man.

It has been ten years since I first took up my post, a young cleric, full of hope. Despite the hardships and the heartache that I witnessed daily, my life was good and I thanked the Lord for setting me on this most rewarding path. Though shocked by the hardships my parishioners had to endure, I continued to spread the good word, though in a protracted and long-winded manner as was my wont. And indeed, there was much work to be done ministering to the spiritual and physical needs of these poor unfortunates and I embraced my calling with all the vigour at my disposal.

However, there came a time when I became aware of a shadow falling over my parish, blocking out the sun that warmed souls and enlightened lives.

The unwitting messenger for this portent of doom was a young woman called Poppy Makepeace. Poppy was an irregular member of my parish, preferring to try her luck in many other cities but always returning here when fortune failed to smile upon her for more than the briefest of moments. I hazarded that she was somewhere in her mid-twenties, but the nature of her life had worked ill upon her features. She claimed to have been a ladies maid until the son of the house had made an un-gentlemanly demand upon her. Her refusal had led to her dismissal upon what she swore was a trumped-up charge of theft. Thus thrown upon the streets she fended for herself as best she could, which, unfortunately, led to a life of petty thieving, drunkenness and lewd behaviour for the price of a bed or a bottle.

The smog had never fully lifted that day and as the short afternoon gave way to early evening shadows I spied Poppy sitting outside a particularly un-salubrious hostelry called the Pump and Crow. She hailed me from across the street and I returned the wave, crossing to see how she fared.

'Hello Poppy,' I said and she cackled and slapped her knee at my presence.

'Father Pete as ever was!' she said. 'Come to save our souls have you, Father?'

'If you wish to be saved, I can set you on the path of redemption without doubt,' I replied.

She cocked her head and studied me closely. 'What say we discuss it over a drop of gin, eh, Father?' she grinned.

I returned the smile, for, despite her faults, Poppy had a charm about her that invited friendship and camaraderie. I held out my hand. 'Come,' I said, 'let me lead you from temptation instead.'

She heaved a sigh but took my hand and let me haul her to her feet regardless. 'Too late for that, Father,' she said. 'But I'll walk a ways with you for old time's sake.'

She linked her arm through mine and I did my best to

steady her wavering gait. We talked of this and that and I enquired if she had lodgings in these perilous times.

'If I can do a bit of business I can get the price of a room and maybe a drop of something to keep the cold out as well,' she said.

I told her that she need not descend to such depths just to secure lodgings and recommended that she present herself at Sanguine House which took in destitute women and gave them food and lodgings of which I had heard good things. She gave me the strangest look and then her mouth curled up in what I can only describe as a sneer.

'Wouldn't catch me anywhere near that place, your Reverence,' she said. 'Neither would you if you knew what goes on behind those doors.'

Thinking she had mistakenly assumed Sanguine House was still plying its former trade as a house of ill repute, I strove to calm her fears and replace them instead with the hope of forgiveness and redemption it now offered under its new owner's most attentive care.

'You need not fear for your safety,' I said. 'Sanguine House is now a refuge for those poor unfortunate souls who find themselves cast adrift upon life's tumultuous seas.'

Still staring deep into my eyes in a most disconcerting manner, she said: 'You don't know do you?'

'Know what?' I asked, perplexed.

She began to laugh then, a loud, raucous sound full as much of relief as with mirth. 'Oh, that's rich, that is. Poor Father Pete. The Devil hisself right under your nose and you don't know!'

Her behaviour now was beginning to vex me. 'If you

have no need of my assistance,' I said in what I confess was a haughty manner, 'then I shall bid you goodnight.' I straightened my cuffs and turned to go on my way, but now it was Poppy who hurried after me and sought to delay my progress.

'Wait,' she said. 'I didn't mean to offend you. You've always been kind to me and now I think I should pay you back for that kindness, though you will curse me to Hell and back for my trouble, but you have to know.'

'What on earth are you babbling about, girl?' I demanded in a curt and offended tone that I promised myself I would do penance for at the earliest opportunity, but Poppy's actions had quite discomfited me.

'Come with me, Father, if you will. If you want to really know what goes on behind those walls, if you think your soul can bear the burden, come with me now.'

Thinking the poor child had quite lost her senses, I decided it best to humour her and we set off through the fog, our footsteps echoing across the cobbles, all other sounds and sights indistinct and muffled as if the whole world had been wrapped in a thick layer of wool. Shadows passed us, but we may as well have been the last two souls to walk this mortal coil. As Poppy led me down back streets and alleyways I quite lost my sense of direction and believed we must be embarked on a fool's errand until the faint glow of a streetlamp showed me that we had come upon a street I recognised full well.

'Why,' I said, 'it's Sanguine House. You have brought me to the very place you swore to never grace with your presence.'

'Just this one time, Father. For I need to show you what I

mean, else you will not believe me.'

I sighed and allowed myself to be led to a side door, away from the main thoroughfare. Here, Poppy paused and placed her ear against the wood, listening intently.

'Why do we not simply enter through the front door?' I asked.

She shushed me vehemently. 'You need to be quiet, Father,' she said. 'Promise me you won't say a word until I give you leave. Promise me.'

With another weary sigh, I gave my assent. Seemingly satisfied that I would be as good as my word, Poppy returned to her vigilant eavesdropping. I could hear no sound of movement from within and, after a short while, Poppy nodded and turned the handle. The door opened easily enough and Poppy ushered me in. We found ourselves in a passageway that ran behind the kitchens. Taking my sleeve, Poppy hurried us along the hallway to a set of stairs that serviced the upper floor. As watchful as a cat, Poppy bade me climb the stairs in her wake until we had reached the first floor landing. The sound of muted voices came from behind a few of the doors but so far we had seen no-one who might mark our presence as strange or unusual. I heard the sound of laughter from behind one door and smiled to myself to think that such good work could inspire such lightness of heart in one whose lot in life had been so pitiful. The sound seemed to spur Poppy to greater haste and she fairly dragged me along the corridor. The carpet underfoot muffled our footsteps until we reached a small door situated at the end of the landing. With a quick look left and right, Poppy pulled open the door and pushed me inside following close on my heels.

The space it led to was too small to be a dormitory room and I assumed it must be a cupboard of some sort. When she closed the door behind her, the interior was pitch black. I started to protest but a sharp dig in my ribs from her elbow reminded me to keep my own counsel. I heard a scurry of movement and then the sound of a match being struck. A candle on a small table flared to life shedding enough light to make out a small, square room furnished with a single armchair that was curiously facing the wall. Aside from the chair and the table, the room was unfurnished and would in fact have been too small to serve any useful function as room at all which bolstered my assumption that this was simply a repository for unwanted articles of furniture. In the feeble light of the candle, I could barely make out Poppy's features. With a warning finger across her lips to ensure my silence, she began to speak in a hushed whisper that was barely audible.

'I did a turn or two here when this was a knocking shop,' she said. 'You think it's changed, Father? Well, you'd be wrong on that score. It's just a different kind of knocking shop now, that's all.'

'Poppy,' I whispered, 'I have no idea what you are talking about. And where are we?'

'They call it the Priest's Hole, Father,' and she gave a small, cynical laugh. 'All the girls knew about this room. You see, some gents are what you might call players and others just like to watch the game if you get my drift.'

I had no idea what she was referring to and was about to say so, when there came the sound of a door opening, so close the rattle of the handle made me start. Poppy grabbed my arm tightly. 'The game's afoot,' she said. 'Quiet now as you value your life.'

With that, she guided me towards the armchair and bade me sit. I did so, perplexed beyond measure. Poppy blew out the candle, plunging us into stygian gloom, but then, to my surprise, the faintest glow of light appeared in front of me. That mystery at least became clear when Poppy reached across and drew back a curtain revealing a small aperture that I assumed led into the room next door. She gently pushed me forward until my nose was resting against the musty smelling wall and my eyes were level with the glimmer of light leeching in from the neighbouring room. I realised then, of course, that this was a simple peephole, disguised on the other side no doubt by some elaborate piece of carving, its sole purpose was to allow the occupant of this chair to spy on the activities in the adjacent apartment. Having no wish to engage in such activity, I made to push myself up from the chair with every intention of quitting this awful place, but Poppy grabbed my shoulders and held me fast.

'Watch,' she hissed, so close to my ear, I could feel the movement of her lips and the spittle of her breath. Even as I girded myself to protest in the strongest possible terms, I heard the sound of muffled voices from within the adjoining room. A door handle rattled and a door closed. The voices were louder now, though still muffled and indistinct, and I assumed that the couple, for it was a man and a woman's voice that I had heard, had entered the room next to where I sat, the room into which I could see via this most wretched contrivance.

'Watch,' Poppy hissed again, her hands like steel upon

my shoulders. Reluctantly, but to my undying shame, I placed my eyes to the peephole, overcome with sinful curiosity. I could see well enough into the room to judge that it had fine furnishings and a large, comfortable bed. This in itself was a puzzle, for this was a simple house providing simple provisions for those women on the lowest rungs of society's ladder. Indeed, the women slept in dormitories and individual rooms were a waste of valuable space, especially one as finely decorated as this seemed to be. True, I had never been inside the house, and I assumed, if indeed I could be said to have thought about it at all, that this was most likely a remnant of its previous persuasion and would, I am sure, have been converted to more useful purpose as soon as time and finances allowed. The fact that it still seemed to be in use was something of a mystery. As these thoughts rumbled through my mind, I watched the scenario in the adjoining room unravel before my eyes.

The man was tall and handsome I dare say in a rugged sort of way and of a distinctly foreign appearance. His companion, a woman, had her back to me and was well dressed. It was not a state that either of them maintained for very long.

As soon as the door was closed behind them, they fell into each other's arms in a long, lingering, passionate and uninhibited embrace. I felt the colour rise to my cheeks as they drew apart, panting, and proceeded to disrobe with unseemly haste, almost ripping the clothes from their bodies in their lust fuelled enthusiasm to be rid of every last scrap of material. Once again, I tried to rise from my chair, but Poppy's grip remained firm.

'You must see it through to the end,' she whispered. 'The very end, though it cost you your sanity if not your soul.'

I had no idea what she was raving about, but frankly, I feared what she might do if I protested too much and so acquiesced to her demands. In the adjoining room, the man and the woman were now both completely naked. The man, still facing me, was solidly built and most obviously aroused. The woman still had her back to me, but I could see that she was well proportioned, her skin smooth and her flesh rounded and firm. The man reached out and touched her body in what I judged from my limited vantage point was a most intimate manner for she shuddered, her flesh rippling with emotion at his caress. She moved quickly then, taking his hand and leading him towards the bed.

'Watch,' Poppy hissed vehemently, and watch I did, though I could scarcely believe my senses. I watched as the woman lay back upon the bed and he climbed between her thighs. Her hands slid between their bodies, grasping him and guiding him into her most intimate part whereupon she clamped her heels around his buttocks pulling and thrusting as he rode her like a stag in rut. Not content with this simple act, they changed position so that she straddled him, their hands, their mouths, indeed every inch of their flesh and every orifice of their bodies brought into play as they screamed and sweated in every imaginable position and many that I had not believed humanly possible or indeed capable of providing any slightest form of human pleasure.

Finally, after what seemed to be to be an eternity in the deepest, darkest bowels of Hell, they fell apart, satiated and exhausted on top of the covers, their lewd nakedness displayed for all to see.

'Wait for it,' Poppy whispered. 'This is where the fun really starts.'

That they would have the energy to perform any other act of perversion did not seem possible and I had no wish to see what that might be if they did, but I had no strength left to fight against her grip, no spirit left to resist her will and so I waited and watched. In a minute or two, the languor that followed their exertions seemed to abate and the man stirred and sat up. I saw him reach into a small cabinet by the side of the bed and withdraw something.

'Now,' Poppy whispered, 'now you will see what this place has become.'

I watched as he sat up and turned to his companion. He leaned towards her and she sat up, taking his face between her palms and kissing him upon the lips. Then she sat back against the pillows and extended her arm towards him. He held her hand, palm uppermost with his left hand. With his right hand he raised the object he had recently retrieved from the bedside cabinet. The glow of the lamps glinted on polished steel and I realised he held a razor in his hand. My muscles jerked involuntarily and I tried again to rise, but Poppy's grip was like iron. Thus imprisoned, I saw him run the wicked blade, tenderly it seemed, across the skin of the woman's forearm. She gave a small shudder and drew in a deep breath. A trickle of blood began to flow, dripping onto her thighs and running onto the bed linen. Then, he cast the razor aside and bent his mouth to the wound, lapping and sucking as though supping on a rare delicacy. Far from agitation or discomfort, she threw back her head and moaned, deep and long, her body writhing in ecstasy as profound as that provoked from their previous coupling. Poppy's voice seemed to come from the depths of a long, dark tunnel.

'There,' she hissed. 'That's what really goes on in this place now. Not just your normal fucking, but the supping of blood by demons from hell. That's the price the girls pay for staying here. And they come back time and time again so they do. They say it's the best ride they ever had but that don't make no difference to me. It ain't worth the price if the demon takes possession of them, steals their souls and makes them want more of what he has to give. This used to be a normal knocking shop and all the better for it if you ask me, but not anymore.'

The vehemence in her voice was caustic, but I paid it no heed. I did not need her opinion or her advice on what I had just witnessed. Suddenly it was all too plain. Here was a demon who preyed on the innocent, stole their blood and corrupted their souls. Though it cost me my own soul, I knew I had to act.

With a final, convulsive thrust, I threw myself up from my chair, knocking it over in my haste. Poppy released her grip, realising that she had unleashed in me a fury she could no longer contain. I was screaming in inarticulate rage as I scrabbled in the darkness for the door. When my hand finally found the handle, I wrenched it open and threw myself into the corridor. I was barely aware of Poppy making a hasty retreat down the back stairs but that was of little concern to me now. Incensed beyond all reason, I burst onto that scene of which I had so recently been an unwilling voyeur. The woman screamed and grasped the sheet and held it to her chin to mask her nakedness and my anger curdled in my stomach to think that she would thus shield herself from God's disciple in such a manner when she had flaunted herself so flagrantly with her illicit paramour. Her companion, on the other hand, showed no such embarrassment and leaped from the bed to face me, quite naked and ostentatiously aroused even now. Having made my entrance, I confess, I had little idea of what I would do next. That decision was taken from me however. The naked foreigner moved with a speed beyond the capabilities of any mortal man I had ever encountered. If that fact alone was not enough to confirm my suspicions that he was less than human, his next action proved that point beyond a shadow of a doubt. Grasping me firmly by the collars of my coat, he lifted me clean off my feet and threw me the length of the room as easily as I might have thrown a child's toy. I landed heavily against the wall, all breath smashed from my lungs, my head ringing with the impact. As I slumped to the floor, my attacker was upon me. He fastened his hands around my throat and lifted me up until my heels were left kicking in mid-air. He exhibited no strain at this feat except an animal snarl that came from his red streaked lips and a fierce glow that turned his eyes into hot coals of animal ferocity. He pressed his grip harder and harder. I clawed ineffectually at his hands and I felt as if my head would explode from the pressure. I had no breath left and my vision began to swim and darken and I uttered a silent prayer that the Good Lord would take my soul into his keeping for I was sure that I had breathed my last. Through the darkening shadows of my senses, I became aware of a voice, shouting and pleading for some leniency on my behalf. The woman. She was tugging at his arm, begging for mercy. Slowly, reluctantly, as I imagined, my assailant relaxed his grip and allowed me to fall to the floor. I lay there, gasping in air as though it were pure ambrosia and coughing, feeling every ache and scrape that had been inflicted upon me as I did so. I was dimly aware of muffled voices as I tried to retrieve my scattered senses. How long I lay in that pitiful huddle I know not, but it must have been some minutes for when I could finally bring my senses to bear, both the woman and her companion were fully dressed. There they stood, a blasphemous Adam and his besmirched Eve. If, as Poppy had intimated, this was truly an emissary of Satan that stood before me I knew my mettle would be put to the supreme test. Not wishing to put myself in harm's way any more than was needed, I fumbled beneath my coat for the crucifix that always hangs around my neck. I held it out and gloried in the knowledge that no spawn of Satan would dare defy the power of goodness that radiated from this most holy of symbols. 'Keep your distance, Sir,' I commanded in a voice that was less stentorian than I had hoped. 'As you can see, I am now prepared for you and will not succumb so easily to your influence.'

To my utter dismay, the creature simply looked at me and smiled.

'He thinks me some myth that can be banished by wood and water,' he sneered, his accent light and almost musical. The woman turned to hush him and moved forward. She closed her fingers over mine and lowered my hand to my side.

'That will do no good,' she whispered. 'This is not as it seems.'

'Come with me now,' I said. 'Come with me and we will pray to the Lord for the safety of your soul and the means to vanquish this most dire evil that walks among us.'

Her companion laughed contemptuously and the woman lowered her eyes from mine. Sadly, she shook her head.

'I cannot do as you ask,' she said softly. 'I must stay here. I must continue my work.'

'The devil's work, you mean,' I spat. 'This Devil has corrupted your mind as surely as he has defiled your flesh! I fear you are lost to the world, but I will pray for you that you may one day seek true repentance and find your way once more back to the one, true, God.'

With that, I edged my way towards the door, forever keeping the crucifix between myself and that emissary of Hell that had brought me so much misery. It was at that moment that the door was wrenched open from the outside and a red-haired ruffian grabbed me by the collar and marched me post haste downstairs where he proceeded to throw me bodily into the street all the while berating me in the most foul language. Once outside I made haste to put as much distance between myself and that sullied establishment as possible. My mind was inflamed as if with fever as I plunged into the smothering fog that enshrouded the city. In truth, I had no idea where I was going but providence from on high guided my footsteps and when I finally came to a halt I was outside my own house. I lost no time in entering and locking and barring the door behind me against any unwanted intrusion. Having thus reached my destination, I threw myself upon my knees and prayed for guidance. When my poor scattered wits proved incapable of receiving that which I so desperately needed, I took to pacing the floor, my mind full of fractured images of the scenario I had witnessed scarce an hour before.

That devils walked the streets, of that I was sure. Their exact nature was unknown to me but it was obvious that they sustained themselves with the blood of the living and exerted a hold upon their victims, who, although still alive, had no will of their own and were forced into depraved and perverted acts they would not otherwise have contemplated, for how else could I explain their actions? And how could I, a humble cleric, hope to oppose such malignant forces? I beat my fists against my brow in an effort to cudgel my poor, ineffectual brain into producing an answer. When none was forthcoming, I thought it would drive me mad and I fell into a deep swoon upon my living room carpet. When I awakened to dawn's pale light my mind was clearer and my course more firmly set. I must expose these creatures for what they were, whatever the cost to myself. With that in mind, I made my way to the nearest police station, this very building where we now sit in fact, but my warnings of evil most vile have fallen on deaf ears and I have no option now but to pray to the Lord God Almighty for his guidance in these most perilous of times. If, by means of this statement, some glimmer of hope may be kindled then my prayers will not be in vain.

Signed: Peter Cheshire

Witnessed by Police Constable William Walter John Colverson.

Abberline closed the file and tugged his ear reflectively, something he was wont to do when thinking.

'What do you think, sir?' Colverson asked.

Abberline looked up as if suddenly remembering the young constable's presence. 'Hmmm? Oh, yes. An unlikely tale as you say.'

'I thought as much, sir. Sorry to have wasted your time.'

'Not at all. I said it was unlikely, but not impossible. As you rightly say, it could just be a misinterpretation of the facts and nothing more. Even so, it seems that two acts of violence occurred at this Sanguine House that bear investigation. Whether they pertain to the Ripper case is something we will not know until we have paid that same establishment a visit. What do you say Colverson? Shall we go?'

*

''Ello ducks. I'm Nancy. What's your name?'

'They call me Frank.' His voice was low and thick with the tones of foreign climes. 'Frank Nasty.'

Emma Smith giggled. 'That's a funny name.'

'It isn't my given name any more than Nancy is yours. It is the closest you English can come to pronouncing my real name.'

''Ow do you know my real name aint Nancy?'

'Those of your type who provide this service are all called Nancy, is that not so? That is why I was told to ask for Nancy at the door. The person who told me this said that "a Nancy would see me right." Unfortunately my first visit was interrupted by a meddlesome cleric.'

'That barmpot! I heard about that.'
'It did rather spoil the mood. Which is why I have returned.'
'Don't worry love, we won't get no interruptions tonight.'
'Let us hope so.'
'So, what is your real name then?'
'Ferenc Nadasdy.'
'Blimey, that's a mouthful! I'll just call you Frank.'
'As you wish. Now, take off your clothes.'

*

In the back parlour of Sanguine House, Sir Francis Varney, tall, sparse and fine featured, sat in deep conversation with Angus Rawshank, a broad, heavily muscled Scot with a thick head of red hair and a fulsome beard as had all the men of his clan down throughout the centuries. Some papers were spread out on the table before them.

'D'ye really think it's him?' Rawshank asked.

Varney nodded. 'There are details in these missives that only he could know.'

'And he's comin' here?'

'So he says. If nothing else, I believe him to be a man of his word.'

Rawshank shook his head and gestured to the fireplace above which a ceremonial Scottish claymore took pride of place. 'If he does, we'll be ready for him. Yon claidheamh-mor is a mite thirsty after all these years.'

Varney smiled. 'I would expect nothing more from a Rawshank. Your ancestor who was my friend as well as my closest ally would be proud of you, but it may not be that simple. We don't even know what he looks like.'

'True enough, but he'll tip his hand soon enough.'

A knock sounded at the front door. Rawshank rose from his chair. 'I'll get it. It's a slow night and we can't afford to turn away custom.'

*

After some muted discussion on the doorstep, Rawshank ushered two visitors into Varney's presence. The one, dressed in plain clothes with a mild, self-effacing appearance, the other a uniformed constable.

'I'm Detective Chief Inspector Abberline. This is Police Constable Colverson.'

'A pleasure to meet you, Chief Inspector, Constable. Won't you sit down? Angus, some refreshments for our guests.'

'Thank you, Sir Francis, but no. We are here on official business I'm afraid, not a social call.'

'Oh, dear, that does sound serious. What can I do to help, Chief Inspector?'

'We've had reports of an altercation that allegedly took place here some nights ago.'

'An altercation? What sort of altercation?'

'A violent assault involving a gentleman of the cloth during which a young woman, so it is claimed, was cut with a knife.'

Rawshank growled. 'It'll be that mad cleric. Him that's always shouting the odds outside. I told you about him, Sir Francis.'

'Oh, yes, so you did. A most unfortunate misunderstanding. The gentleman of the cloth in question has formed an unfortunate opinion of Sanguine House, probably based on its previous use as a house of dubious moral purposes. I can assure you that is no longer the case. These days, Sanguine House provides shelter and succour for young ladies whose good fortune has deserted them momentarily. As the name suggests it is a place of cheerfulness and hope.'

'Perhaps so, Sir Francis, but does the term "sanguine" not also refer to blood?'

Varney smiled. 'Touche, Chief Inspector,' he said.

'And the events on the night in question?' Abberline pressed.

'One of our young ladies was being visited by her cousin. A most respectable young man of means who wished to take her under his wing. The clerical gentleman managed to gain access to the house by some uncertain method and misread the situation.'

'And the blood he claims to have witnessed?'

'Oh, a mere trifle. The young lady was engaged in some needlework and pricked her finger. Her cousin was attending to her wound when Father Cheshire – that is his name I believe – burst into the room and started a ruckus. Angus here had to eject him I'm afraid. He was upsetting our other guests.'

'Aye, that's right,' Rawshank affirmed. 'I tossed the old bible thumper out on his ear.'

'Gently, of course, Angus.'

'Aye, right enough. I escorted him from the premises. Smartish.'

'This young lady and her cousin,' Abberline said. 'Are we able to speak to them in person, to confirm their version of events?'

'Alas, no,' Varney smiled. 'The very next day, the young man withdrew his cousin from our care. I believe he said he had plans for a sojourn in Europe so that the young lady could catch up with her interrupted education, isn't that so, Angus?'

'Aye, that's what he said. A very long and immediate sojourn at that.'

'How very convenient,' Abberline murmured.

'Convenient, Chief Inspector? How so?'

'If I may speak plainly, Sir Francis?'

'Of course.'

'Very well. Despite your assertions otherwise, I do not believe Sanguine House has changed its purpose at all. It was then and is now, a brothel.'

Rawshank made a rumbling noise, but Varney raised a hand. 'Go on, Chief Inspector,' he said.

'Routine patrols of the area suggest an abnormal amount of gentlemen callers frequenting these premises at all hours of the day and night. I do not believe that their purpose is solely one of familial duty or Christian charity. I do believe, however, that Father Cheshire witnessed more than a mere pinprick by an awkward seamstress and, for reasons of your own, you are choosing to hide that fact. I further believe that this incident may be connected to a series of brutal murders and if I discover that you are wilfully obstructing the police in the furtherance of their duty ...'

At that moment a scream rent the air, loud enough to wake the dead, not that it did Emma Smith much good. For a split second all four men froze and then, as one, dashed out into the hall.

On the upstairs landing, a young woman, dressed only in her underwear, cowered against the bannister. One door stood open. In the doorway stood a figure. Stocky, bearded, dark haired, his arms, hands and shirt covered in blood. In his right hand he held a bloody knife. Other doors were beginning to open, their inhabitants drawn by the commotion. Young women in various stages of undress and, mainly older, men equally dishevelled but trying desperately to re-assemble their full attire, quickly spilled onto the landing.

Glancing quickly from side to side, the man that Emma Smith had briefly known as Frank Nasty, summed up his possible escape options and chose the most direct.

With a snarl, he vaulted over the bannister and dropped to the hall floor some twenty feet below. Landing impressively upon his feet, he rose up uninjured and charged the four men blocking his exit.

Colverson was the first to meet his charge, countering the knife with his stout, oak night stick. A hefty blow to Nasty's right arm caused him to drop the knife with a howl of pain. A swift follow through to the side of his head knocked the man back but did not fell him. Momentarily stunned by this unexpected result from a tried and true tactic for disarming an enraged assailant, Colverson left himself vulnerable to a prodigious shove that sent him careering across the hall to slam into the wall hard enough to crack the plaster. Seizing his opportunity, Rawshank closed on their assailant from behind, gripping him in a bear hug that pinned his arms to his side. All to no avail. Nasty broke Rawshank's grip with almost childlike ease, heaving the muscular Scot over his shoulder to send him cannoning into Abberline. Both men went sprawling. Picking up the knife, Nasty faced Varney who closed with the madman demonstrating surprising strength for one so slender of build and forcing Nasty back. Using Varney's own momentum against him, Nasty fell back, kicking upwards into Varney's stomach as he did so, lifting his opponent high over his head to slam into the floor. Springing to his feet, Nasty growled: 'Not like this, Varney. Your end will not be so easy. I will return to finish this.'

So saying he made for the door only to be met by Abberline, revolver in hand.

'Drop the knife,' Abberline commanded. 'You're under arrest.'

Nasty simply grinned. In a movement too swift to follow, his left hand lashed out, knocking Abbeline's gun aside and instigating a reflexive pull on the trigger that sent a bullet crashing into the wall. In the same instant, Nasty's right hand thrust the knife deep into Abberline's stomach. As the policeman fell to the floor in a pool of blood, Nasty gained the front door and vanished into the night.

*

It was a singularly unique experience for Detective Chief Inspector Abberline. To awaken in a whore's bed surrounded by a member of the aristocracy, a red-headed Scotsman, Abberlines own ashen faced constable and several of the aforementioned whores whose scanty attire left little to the imagination.

'What ...?' was the only thing his addled mind could summon up.

'Ah, Chief Inspector. So good of you to join us.' Varney smiled.

Abberline attempted to sit up and winced as a stab of pain lanced through his stomach.

'No, no,' Varney said. 'Do not attempt to rise. You need rest Chief Inspector and lots of it.' Varney laid his hands upon Abberline's shoulders and, with a surprisingly firm but gentle pressure, eased the policeman back onto his pillows.

'You have sustained an injury,' Varney told him. 'Thankfully it is not life threatening. Not now, anyway.'

Abberline looked down to see his shirt covered in blood. A rent in the fabric the seeming source of his discomfort.

'I have arranged a carriage for you,' Varney told him. 'It is waiting outside this very moment with instructions to take you home where you must rest. A good hot toddy maybe to aid sleep and in the morning you will feel much better I assure you. Now, if you will allow us to assist you to your carriage, all will be well.'

With no strength to object, Abberline allowed Rawshank and Colverson to support him downstairs and out to the carriage. The soiled doves who resided at Sanguine House fluttered around this strange entourage, most red eyed from crying, the rest in various stages of agitation, but Abberline's mind was too fogged to make much sense of events.

*

Once inside the carriage with Colverson beside him, the coachman flicked his whip and the horses moved away.

Abberline took a deep breath, feeling his wound twinge as he did so.

'Now, Colverson,' he said. 'What the hell just happened?'

Some colour had returned to the young constable's face but his eyes still had a haunted cast about them. 'I'm not sure I rightly know, sir,' he said.

'Then tell me what you do know and we will start from there.'

'Well, it started with a scream.'

'I remember. And in the hall. The man with the knife.'

'That's right, sir. That jump from the landing. I felt sure he'd do himself some damage. A broken leg for sure, but up he comes and goes for us like a madman.' Colverson patted his truncheon, now safely tucked into his belt. 'I got him two good whacks with Betsy here and that's usually enough to take the fight out of anyone.'

'You call your night stick Betsy?'

'Named after my grandmother, sir. She was a redoubtable woman and no mistake.'

'I'm sure she was. Carry on, Colverson. What happened next?'

'Well, the blighter just shrugged it off and shoved me so hard I fairly sailed ten feet across the hall to slam into the wall so hard I thought my ribs would break.'

'I have vague recollections of all this, Colverson. The miscreant then knocked us about like tenpins before uttering a threat against Sir Francis.'

'That's correct, sir. Just before he stabbed you and ran out the door.'

Abberline nodded. 'Why didn't you give chase? You may have been able to apprehend him.'

'I would have, sir, but I was too concerned for your welfare.'

'Your concern is appreciated, Colverson, but duty comes first. Besides, it was obviously a flesh wound, otherwise I wouldn't be sitting here talking to you.'

Colverson shook his head. 'That's just it, sir. It wasn't a flesh wound. It was serious. You lost so much blood I feared you would die on the spot. I believe you would have done so if not for Sir Francis.'

'Sir Francis?'

Colverson lowered his eyes. 'What he did ... I've never seen the like. I'm still not sure I believe it and I saw it with my own eyes.'

'What did he do, Colverson?'

'Well, he looked at your wound. It was gushing blood something awful. He said he had to do something drastic or you were a goner. Then, he pulls this knife from his pocket. A real fancy silver article it was. I wasn't happy with the look of that and I tried to stop him but Rawshank held me back in a grip like iron. Anyway, Sir Francis used the knife before I could stop him. But not on you. On himself.'

'On himself?'

'That's right, sir. He rolled up his sleeve and slashed his own forearm. Then he leant over you and dripped his own blood into your mouth.'

'Good God!'

'I couldn't see what good that would do, but he kept feeding you drops of blood and slowly the wound ...'

'What about the wound?'

'It began to close.'

'Close? Impossible.'

'So I thought, but see for yourself, sir.'

Abberline parted his torn, blood-stained shirt. Apart from a pinkish smear of dried blood the flesh was smooth and unblemished save for a small scar about two inches long as if from a wound long since healed. He probed the spot with tentative fingers. Tender for sure but no real pain. Abberline stared at Colverson.

'And you are sure that this was an open wound prior to my being administered ...blood?'

'I swear on my mother's life, sir. You could have fitted two fingers in it before, but after, it just sort of ...closed.'

'Remarkable.'

Abberline sat back and closed his eyes. A feeling of immense fatigue washed over him and he could easily have fallen asleep, but suddenly he jerked awake and sat forward.

'The victim!' he said. 'What of the victim? Who had that madman butchered?'

Colverson shook his head sadly. 'Beyond saving I'm afraid, sir. One of the girls who lived there. Emma Smith by name. Cut up something awful. Dead before we could get to her.'

'Then we must go back. Why did you not summon assistance? What were you thinking, man?'

Colverson made calming motions with his hands. I thought of all that, sir, but I wasn't allowed to.'

'Not allowed? You are an officer of the law, Colverson. It's your duty.'

'I know, sir, but I was overruled.'

'By whom? Not by Sir Francis surely? He may be a peer of the realm but he does not dictate to Scotland Yard nor does he have the authority to overrule our decisions in these matters.'

'Quite so, sir, but there is one who does.'

'And who might that be? Not the Commissioner, surely? Don't tell me he was one of the "gentlemen" availing himself of the services provided by Sanguine House?'

Colverson smiled at the thought. 'No, sir, not the Commissioner. Someone even further up the chain of command.'

'Further ...? Who on earth do you mean?'

'The Home Secretary, sir. The 1st Viscount Llandaff PC KC. Mr. Henry Matthews.'

*

'The Home Secretary?' For several seconds Abberline was lost for words. 'You mean he was there, at Sanguine House?'

'Not to start with, sir, but Sir Francis sent for him.'

'Sent for him? The owner of a brothel "sends" for the Home Secretary and he obliges?'

'He didn't seem too happy about it, sir, but, yes. Even as Sir Francis was tending to yourself, he told Rawshank to send a runner to fetch "you know who". That's how he referred to him at that point. I had no idea who he meant, but in the time it took to get you settled in Maisie's bed – that's the name of the young lady whose room you were taken to – a nice enough young thing, someone you wouldn't expect to be plying that sort of trade.'

'Never mind Maisie! What happened next?'

'Well, as soon as I was sure you were recovering, I insisted on seeing the scene of the crime. Awful it was, sir. Equally as bad as Mary Kelly. And I was all for summoning reinforcements as you rightly say I should have done, but Sir Francis physically prevented me from leaving the house. He is remarkably strong, sir, for one so slight of build and our exchange of views became quite heated. It was as I was contemplating using Betsy to reinforce my argument when the Home Secretary arrived.'

'You're sure it really was the Home Secretary?'

'Absolutely, sir. I've seen his photograph in the papers often enough and that time when the Commissioner held a function to celebrate his appointment I was part of the honour guard. It was him right enough.'

'And what did he say?'

'Well, he looked at the crime scene. Briefly. Then he had a quiet word with Sir Francis. After that he told me that this was no longer a case for Scotland Yard and I was to make no formal report on the matter. Any further action to be taken was the sole province of Sir Francis who was acting with the government's full authority. And then he left. The rest you know, sir.'

'Astounding.'

'Sir Francis said that he would provide additional information tomorrow or whenever you were feeling up to it and made these arrangements to see you safely home.'

'Yes. Home. That is where I believe I belong at this moment …Oh Dear Lord!'

'What is it, sir? Is your wound playing up? Should I get the driver to take us to the hospital instead?'

'No, no. No hospital. My wound is remarkably fine, but I've just had a thought.'

'What would that be, sir?'

'How am I going to explain all this to my wife?'

*

As events turned out, Detective Chief Inspector Abberline did not have to explain himself to his wife that night. That task fell to a visibly nervous Police Constable Colverson. During the remainder of their journey, Abberline had succumbed to another bout of extreme fatigue and Colverson had to almost carry the Inspector from the carriage to his own front door where they were met by Mrs. Emma Abberline who herself succumbed to a state of agitation upon seeing her blood spattered, semi-conscious spouse. It is a testimony to her strength of spirit that she roused herself instantly into action of the most practical sort. Eliciting Colverson's aid in transporting Abberline upstairs to his bed, she gave strict instructions that the Constable should remain downstairs whilst she made her husband comfortable because she intended to hear chapter and verse on the events that had led to such a necessity and, make no mistake about it, Colverson would provide that information or suffer the consequences. As he waited shifting nervously from foot to foot and wishing for nothing more than his own bed, Colverson reflected on the fact that, despite her slight frame and delicate features, Emma Abberline was a formidable woman. In truth, Colverson found most women formidable and, in consequence, unnerving, most having the innate ability to undermine his authority as a guardian of the law. Give me a knife wielding maniac any day of the week, he thought to himself. At least I know how to deal with those.

Colverson's wait was finally over. Emma Abberline presented herself before him and, ever the perfect hostess, asked if he would like some tea or a sandwich perhaps? Caught off guard by this generosity, Colverson muttered that he was fine, thank you very much and really should be going. In that he was to be thwarted. Emma Abberline seated herself and demanded an explanation as to why her husband was returned to her semi-conscious, covered in blood and yet seemed to have no discernible wound save for a faint scratch that she had never seen before.

Colverson felt his face redden and stammered something to the effect that it was a police matter and, he felt sure, the Inspector would answer any questions she may have in the morning.

'Not good enough, constable,' Emma told him. 'I accept that your and Frederick's profession requires a degree of confidentiality and puts you in various forms of danger on a daily basis, but I feel that these events are sufficiently strange to warrant more than being a "police matter".

Colverson had to agree and logic told him that to dissemble more would only prolong his agony and may lead to serious trouble should Mrs. Abberline take her concerns to a higher authority. After all, he reasoned, if you can't trust the discretion of a Chief Inspector's wife who can you trust? Thus decided, he relayed the evening's events as best he could, pausing only when the suspect had made a dash for freedom.

'But what about Frederick's wound?' Emma wanted to know. 'He seems relatively sound now, but something very strange has happened, of that I am sure. If the blood on his clothes came from his wound, how is it that there is no sign of such? And if so severely wounded, how did he survive?'

'That would be down to Sir Francis, Maam. He administered ...first aid.'

'First aid? I belong to the Women's Movement, Constable and am conversant with first aid. There is nothing in the manual that comes under that heading that could have staunched such an injury. Nothing outside the realms of fiction that is.' She paused. 'Oh!'

'Oh, Maam?'

'One moment, Constable.'

Colverson watched, somewhat bemused, as Emma Abberline opened up a large sewing basket and began rooting around in its contents until she acquired that which she sought.

She turned back to him clutching a slim volume to her bosom, a faint blush colouring her cheeks.

'My husband knows nothing of this, Constable, so you must swear to me that you will not breathe a word of what I am about to disclose.'

Now it was Colverson's turn to blush, his mind running rampant with what his superior's wife might be about to disclose. 'I'm not sure I ...' he began.

'Swear to me, Constable, that this is just between the two of us.'

'Very well, maam. I swear,' Colverson capitulated.

'I am a member of the Gentlewomen's Reading Group.'

'As well as the Women's Movement?'

'I belong to many such groups. My husband's duties keep

him busy at all hours of the day and night and a woman needs to find activities that will keep her physical and mental faculties sharp, do you not agree, Constable?'

'Oh, most definitely, maam,' Colverson muttered, praying fervently that she would not go on to enumerate the many ways in which these activities impacted upon her physical and mental wellbeing. Some things, he reasoned, are best kept between man and wife.

'Our group meets once a month,' Emma continued, 'to read and discuss works of literary merit. Our reading matter covers a wide range from the classics to more modern works including some that you might call ... esoteric in nature.' Here she thrust forward the volume that she had been guarding so jealously. 'This is our latest item for discussion. I fear Fredeick may deem it frivolous and unsuitable for gentlewomen, but I believe, as do we all, that it has considerable literary merit.'

Colverson tentatively took the proffered item.

'The Vampire's Torment or The Blood Tryst by Oliver Wendell Reed?' he read. 'A penny dreadful?'

'Indeed not, Constable,' Emma told him firmly. 'This is a stylish and accomplished work dealing with issues of fidelity and loss using gothic imagery and mystical metaphors to underscore the torment and trials of the human condition. It is a work of searing beauty crafted by a fine intellect. All the ladies of the reading group agree it is so.'

'If you say so, maam. But I'm still not sure ...'

'Look here, Constable,' Emma snatched the book back and thumbed through the pages. 'Here,' she said, 'page ninety-seven. The protagonist, Count Orloff, is on the verge of losing the love of his life, Lady Nancy Carstairs, who has been gravely wounded by the dastardly villain, Montgomery Cavendish. The Count knows the only way to save her is by revealing his true nature, which he has pledged never to do lest it leads her to reject him for something which he has no control over.

Read.'

Emma thrust the book back into his hands and Colverson reluctantly read the passage indicated. It was late and he was tired and not a little traumatised. More than anything he wanted his bed not to be reading some trashy romantic concoction, but duty held him fast and he began to read.

Emma waited patiently. When Colverson looked up she saw in his eyes that her surmise had been correct.

'This is ...' Colverson began.

'I'm right, aren't I?' Emma interrupted. 'Count Orloff saves Lady Nancy's life by opening his veins and sharing his life's blood with her. That same blood that has life enhancing qualities. That is how Sir Francis saved Frederick's life isn't it?'

'It's ... remarkably similar, maam. But how ...'

'How Mr. Wendell Reed came to know of these individuals I do not know, but the facts are plain. Count Orloff is able to accomplish this feat because he is a member of an ancient fraternity known as Vampires. If Sir Francis is also able to duplicate such a feat he too must be a vampire!'

*

Colverson spent what little remained of the night in fretful slumber, waking with the dawn, his mind still awhirl with images both real and imaginary. What had begun as a simple case of chasing a brutal mass murderer now seems to have degenerated into a tale of supernatural bogeymen involving Government officials at the highest level. Whatever the eventual outcome, Colverson had his duty to perform. Washed, shaved and attired in his uniform, he set out for Whitechapel Police Station. It was as he approached that palace of justice that he saw the sleek, black, carriage pull up to the kerb. He recognised the driver as Angus Rawshank and, as he drew nearer, the carriage door opened and Sir Francis

Varney alighted with a spring in his step and a smile on his face.

'Ah, Constable,' he said. 'I'm glad I caught you. Had you entered these august portals you may have been tempted to inform your colleagues of last evening's events despite the Home Secretary's instructions to the contrary and that would never do.'

'Would it not?'

'Absolutely not. Now, if you would be so kind as to enter my carriage I have a little outing planned which will put things in perspective and set your mind at rest. Shall we?'

'But the Inspector ...?'

'Still sound asleep I would imagine. He has been through rather a lot. Never mind. We shall call for him en-route. By the time we arrive I feel sure he will be back in the land of the living if you'll pardon the expression. Now, if you will, we have a rather important train to catch later and we cannot be late.'

*

True to Sir Francis' prediction, Detective Chief Inspector Abberline was still fast asleep when the sleek black carriage deposited its occupants at his front door. Emma Abberline on the other hand was very much awake, her mind over-run with images of a tall, mysterious member of the aristocracy who wielded powers far beyond those that most of us would aspire to. Nor was she disappointed when she opened her front door to be confronted by the smiling countenance of Sir Francis Varney.

'Mrs. Abberline I presume? So pleased to make your acquaintance. I am Sir Francis Varney. I believe the good Constable may have mentioned me in passing. May we come in?'

Once safely ensconced in the Abberline's small but cozy

living room, a pot of tea and a plate of sugar biscuits at their disposal, Emma could not resist asking the question that had been burning through her mind all night.

'Begging your pardon, Sir Francis,' she said, 'but Constable Colverson tells me I have you to thank for saving my husband's life and for that I must thank you from the bottom of my heart.'

Varney waved her thanks aside with a smile, a sugar biscuit half way to his lips. 'Think nothing of it, dear lady. It was the least I could do for one of Scotland Yard's finest officers.'

Emma chewed her lip. 'Yes,' she ventured, 'but the method you employed was somewhat unusual was it not?'

Varney chewed ruminatively on his biscuit. 'Needs must as they say,' he replied. 'I am only too thankful that I was successful.'

'Yes,' Emma ploughed on doggedly, 'but it does raise a question which, forgive my impertinence, I feel compelled to ask you.'

'And what might that be, dear lady?'

'Are you one of "them"?'

Varney smiled. 'I am many things Mrs. Abberline, most of which can be categorised as "them". To which particular "them" do you refer?'

Emma screwed up her courage and came right out with it. 'A vampire.'

There was a moment's silence in the room. Varney pondered for a second and then smiled his most beguiling smile. 'My dear lady,' he said, 'what do you know of such things?'

Emma produced her copy of "The Vampire's Torment" from the pocket of her dress. 'Only what I have read in this,' she said.

Varney's smile broadened as he rose slowly to his feet. 'The Vampire's Torment! I've not seen a copy for years. Did you enjoy it?'

Taken aback by his reaction, Emma stammered: 'Very much so. As did the ladies of my reading group. Oliver Wendell Reed is a writer of such delicacy, such passion, such understanding of the human condition. We wept openly over the plight of poor Count Orloff and the depth of his love for Lady Nancy.'

'Really? You found him a sympathetic character despite the nature of his condition?'

'Most assuredly so. Despite his affliction, he is the most romantic, most human creation in all of literature.'

Colverson watched this exchange with bemusement, resigning himself that this particular scene must simply be allowed to play itself out and helped himself to another sugar biscuit, not having had time for a proper breakfast.

Varney clapped his hands in delight. 'You flatter me Mrs. Abberline, you really do.'

Emma looked momentarily confused. 'You, Sir Francis? I'm not sure I understand.'

Varney gently took the novel from her hand. 'Oliver Wendell Reed,' he said, 'is simply a pseudonym. This humble tale that has so enchanted you and the ladies of your reading group is actually my own work.'

Colverson choked on a sugar biscuit but no-one seemed to notice. Emma's eyes widened and he mouth fell open. 'You?' she finally managed. 'You are Oliver Wendell Reed?'

'In person madam, and you have my most heartfelt thanks for your unsolicited praise for my efforts when most reaction has been to relegate it to the realms of doggerel or some penny dreadful.'

Emma cast a quick, furtive glance at Colverson but he pretended not to notice. For a second, Emma was torn between the joy of meeting her literary hero and the need to press him further on the most important issue that lay before them.

'I speak only the heartfelt truth, Sir Francis, as regards this most marvellous creation, but you still haven't answered my question. Are you a vampire?'

'Yes, I'd rather like to know that as well.'

They all looked up at this new voice to see Detective Chief Inspector Abberline standing in the doorway.

'More importantly,' he said, 'I'd like to know if I am now one also.'

Varney rose and offered Abberline his seat which the Inspector gratefully accepted.

'What leads you to believe that you may be a vampire Chief Inspector?' Varney asked.

'Imbibing the blood of a vampire is the traditional way for a mortal to be "turned" is the expression I believe.'

'That is one way, certainly.'

Emma Abberline gave a small cry and clasped her hand to her mouth.

'But fear not, dear lady,' Varney said reassuringly. 'Many other factors need to align for that to happen. In your husband's case, he simply received enough of an infusion to restore him to health and nothing more.'

'Then you admit that you are a vampire?' Emma asked.

'That is undeniably true,' Varney smiled. 'As your husband's return to health and fitness surely attests, but your knowledge of vampire traits is somewhat surprising Chief Inspector.'

'Yes,' Emma said, 'that puzzles me as well. I didn't know you had an interest in such things, Frederick.'

'Nor I you,' Abberline replied and Emma had the good grace to blush. 'As for myself, my interest stems from a case some time ago. You remember, Colverson? The case of Spring Heeled Jack.'

'Why yes, sir, of course.'

'We had reports of a demonic-like creature,' Abberline continued. 'He would jump out of the shadows and cut the clothes of young women with a blade of some sort. The papers named him Spring Heeled Jack after a legendary succubus who climbed into women's rooms at night and drained them of their life force by sitting on their chest.'

Emma made a face. 'Ugh!' she said. 'How revolting.'

'Indeed. Although I doubted the supernatural element of the crimes, I felt it only right that I researched their mythic origins in case it should be pertinent. In learning about the succubus and the incubus I also acquired a passing knowledge of the vampire legend.'

'And did this Spring Heeled Jack have more mortal origins, Chief Inspector?' Varney asked.

'He did indeed, and it was Colverson here who cracked the case.'

'I merely did my part, sir,' Colverson muttered modestly.

'Nonsense. Credit where it is due, Colverson. Tell us the rest of the story if you will. I fear I am still a trifle fatigued.'

Colverson cleared his throat. 'Well,' he said, 'as all the young ladies who had been attacked gave a very similar description of their assailant, it was hard to dismiss his appearance as anything but factual. So, I sat them down with a police artist who drew up a likeness. Since it seemed unlikely that anyone could look like this naturally I reasoned he might be in disguise. I took the sketch to all the theatrical costumiers I could find and compiled a list of all the likely make-up needed to effect such a disguise. From there it was simply a matter of finding out who had purchased such a combination.'

'And that led you to the culprit?' Varney asked.

'Yes sir. An out of work actor called Claude Merrill. He had plans for a one-man show based on the legend and this was his way of drumming up some advance publicity. A daft scheme if ever there was one.'

'But excellent police work all the same, Colverson,' Abberline said.

'I agree,' Varney said. 'Bravo Constable. Which only confirms my thoughts on how to proceed with this current situation.'

'Which is?' Abberline said.

Varney consulted a gold pocket watch and frowned. 'Something that I will explain in full, but only once we are on the move. That is, if you are feeling up to it, Inspector? If not, I am sure that Constable Colverson will make an excellent substitute on your behalf.'

Abberline levered himself to his feet. 'Apart from some lingering lethargy, I am remarkably fit, considering.'

'Excellent news. Shall we proceed, gentlemen?'

Emma stepped forward. 'Sir Francis, before you go, I have a favour to ask you.'

'For you, my dear, anything that is within my power, but please be quick.'

'Would you do me the honour of addressing my reading group? The ladies would be most thrilled.'

'Emma, really!' Abberline said, but Varney simply smiled and waved his objection away.

'It would be my absolute pleasure Mrs. Abberline. As soon as this matter is finished with I would be delighted to do as you ask. For now, we have an important rendezvous at Waterloo Station, Chief Inspector and we must not be late.'

*

As he always did when in need of solace and guidance in the face of life's many conundrums and problems, Father Peter Cheshire sought answers in the text to which he had dedicated his life: The Holy Bible. It had never let him down, but the unspeakable act he had witnessed in that house of sin made him doubt, for just a fraction of a second, the faith that had been his bedrock and his comfort all his life. How can mortal man hope to counteract such blasphemous actions perpetrated by a creature who cannot truly be called a man? He prayed for answers on his knees countless hours until he was too weak and wracked with pain to stand, but no answers were forthcoming. Hobbling back to his humble dwelling he delved once more into the sacred text, more in hope than expectation. And then he saw it. Leviticus 17:11 shone a light on his dilemma:

For the life of a creature is in the blood, and I have given it to you to make atonement for yourselves on the altar; it is the blood that makes atonement for one's life. Therefore I say to the Israelites, "None of you may eat blood, nor may an alien living among you eat blood."

Yes, God's precious gift of blood must not be tainted by being consumed by any mortal or alien being and any who do so are evil personified. This evil must be cast out, but how? It was Psalms 89:46

Fire goes before the Lord and burns up his adversaries all around

and Luke 3: 16

Let your fire be in my hands to heal the sick and cast out

devils. Let your fire burn in my eyes, my heart, my belly, my mouth and my feet

that showed him the way.

It was then that Father Peter Cheshire knew. Knew beyond a shadow of a doubt how this task may be accomplished. Knew also that he and he alone was the chosen one. The Good Lord had chosen him to be in this place and this time. The Good Lord had given this knowledge to him and him alone. He, Peter Cheshire, must make the ultimate sacrifice to rid the world of the demon spawn that stalked the streets of London. To make the streets safe once again the evil must be purged from existence.

Purged by fire.

*

As Varney's carriage conveyed them to Waterloo, Varney explained the history and evolution of vampirism and the purpose served by those women known as Nancy's. He gave details of the Blood Covenant and its purpose in neutralising and combatting those threats to the realm that fell beyond normal military or policing methods. He gave details of the life and death of Ferenc Nadasdy and his own involvement in those events, expressing the theory that this was the cause of their current troubles. Colverson listened with the wide-eyed fascination of a schoolboy. Abberline, despite his personal experience of the last twenty-four hours was less inclined to absolute belief.

'A fascinating tale, Sir Francis,' he said, 'but where is the proof?'

Varney spread his hands. 'Sitting right before me,' he said.

Abberline shook his head. 'I admit that I cannot explain how you accomplished this transformation in my fortunes and I am forever in your debt as a result, but that only supports one fraction of the tale you have just recounted. Without further investigation it is impossible to know if there might be a more scientific or mundane explanation.'

'You are a hard man to convince, Chief Inspector.' Varney smiled. 'I like that. Perhaps the meeting we are about to attend will help to convince you. I hope it does because I think we would be a formidable team if we pooled our resources. But, if it does not ...' he shrugged, 'then we will part company and no more need be said on the matter. Does that seem fair?'

Abberline nodded. 'It does. But you still haven't told us the purpose of our journey.'

At that moment the carriage pulled to a stop at Waterloo Station.

'We have arrived, Chief Inspector. Soon all will be made clear. If you would like to follow me gentlemen.'

*

Soon the three men found themselves on Platform 3, Waterloo Station. The platform was devoid of any passengers and staff, a most unusual occurrence. A private train stood patiently on the tracks. As Varney checked his watch, a carriage door opened. 'Right on time,' Varney murmured. 'Please, step aboard gentlemen where some, if not all, of your questions will be answered.'

Inside, the carriage was fitted out as a sumptuous drawing room, with comfortable chairs and sofas, elegant carved tables and a fine assortment of alcoholic beverages with crystal decanters and glasses. One other item it also contained that was, if anything, even more impressive. A man in crisp military uniform, keen eyed and hawk nosed, his dark hair swept back from a high brow. He stood with hands clasped behind his back as immobile as a statue. His was, presumably, the hand that had opened the carriage door since not another soul was in attendance. Both Abberline and Colverson stopped dead in their tracks, staring in wide eyed wonder at this stern apparition before them. Colverson plucked at Abberline's sleeve. 'Sir?' he whispered. 'Isn't that ...'

Abberline nodded. In an equally soft tone he said: 'Prince Albert of Saxe-Coburg and Gotha. Prince Consort to her majesty Queen Victoria.'

'But isn't he ...'

'Dead for nearly thirty years.'

The slamming of the carriage door did something to break the spell that held them mesmerised but not enough to keep them from stealing covert glances in the silent soldier's direction. Varney swept his hand towards the display of refreshments on offer. 'Now, can I offer you a drink?' he said. Abberline shook his head. 'A trifle early for me,' he said. 'Besides, I am on duty.'

Varney nodded. 'Good man,' he said. 'Duty always comes first, eh? And you, Constable?'

'No thank you, sir.'

'Excellent. Well, do sit down at least.'

Abberline sat in one of the heavily embroidered armchairs and Varney pulled up its twin and sat opposite him. Colverson elected to stand behind Abberline's chair, his hand on his night stick, just in case, his eyes on swivels, not trusting their veracity, but determined to miss no detail, however small to explain the phenomenon they appeared to be witnessing.

'Am I to take it,' Varney continued, 'that we understand each other, Chief Inspector? That you will allow me to continue my mission and bring this affair to a conclusion without any additional involvement from the police?'

Abberline paused for a second and then spoke in a soft, precise voice. 'Gentlemen,' he said, 'I pride myself on having as much humour as the next man, but I fail to see the entertainment in such an elaborate hoax as this.'

Varney frowned. 'What do you mean, Chief Inspector,' he said.

'Merely that your supposition is preposterous. I have no idea of your real standing or what your possible motives might be, but I assure you that Scotland Yard will bring this Ripper fellow to justice without resorting to hocus-pocus or the stuff of fairy tales.'

Before Varney could respond, Abberline rose to his feet and made to leave. 'I bid you good day, gentleman,' he said as he opened the carriage door.

'Leaving now would be most unwise, Detective Abberline. Stay a while longer that I may attempt to convince you in person.'

The voice came from behind him and was irrefutably female. Abberline spun round, but only Varney, Colverson and the soldier met his gaze. Varney pointed towards the corner of the carriage ceiling. 'A speaking tube,' he explained. 'It is linked to the adjoining carriage. The person in that carriage can hear everything we say and, as you now realise, can communicate with us when they so desire.'

'But who ...?' Abberline began.

'Perhaps it would be best if we were to show you,' Varney said. He nodded to his military accomplice who opened the door that would lead to the adjoining compartment. 'After you, Chief Inspector,' he said.

After a moment's hesitation, Abberline strode towards the door, his curiosity piqued and his hand resting in his coat pocket where the comforting heft of his service revolver bolstered his courage. He stepped through into a compartment much the same as he had exited, closely followed by Colverson. Its sole occupant sat in a large, comfortable armchair and fixed him with a stern and implacable stare. Abberline froze on the spot, his mouth opened in wonder. There, before him sat none other than the former Princess Alexandrina Victoria of Kent, better known as Queen Victoria of the United Kingdom.

If Abberline's mouth gaped and his eyes bulged, he can, perhaps, be forgiven this lapse in etiquette, under so unusual a set of circumstances. When his vocal chords once again responded to his mental urging, it was only to utter: 'Your majesty ... I ...'

The monarch of his homeland waved away his mutterings. 'We will dispense with formalities, detective,' she told him. 'My presence here is simply to affirm that the information provided to you by Sir Francis is true. Sir Francis anticipated your scepticism and was reluctant to waste such a potentially important asset as yourself because you could not bring yourself to embrace matters other than those normally encountered by the constabulary.' She paused and studied Abberline's face. When his expression did not change, nor did he utter a single syllable, she nodded and continued. 'There are many things in this world, detective, that are beyond rational explanation. Sir Francis and his associates have been most effective in dealing with such matters and securing the safety of the realm with no fuss or bother and no need to alarm my subjects with their methods or their results. Now that you have my affirmation as to the veracity of these matters, can I trust in your discretion and your co-operation should any future need arise?'

Abberline stared into those implacable, cold, eyes and said the only thing possible under the circumstances. 'Of course, m'aam. It shall be my honour to serve your majesty in whatever capacity you require.'

'Splendid. Sir Francis will see you out.'

*

Not another word was spoken until the three men were safely ensconced once more in Varney's carriage.

'So, Chief Inspector,' Varney broke the silence. 'Has that meeting changed your views on the subject of vampires?'

Abberline let out a long, whispering sigh. 'It is certainly compelling that Her Majesty has such an unshakeable belief in such things, but I would still require more empirical proof if I were to present it before a judge.'

Unable to contain himself any longer, Colverson blurted: 'Was that really His Royal Highness, Prince Albert?'

'Constable!' Abberline chastised. 'That is not the sort of question it is proper to ask. But, under the circumstances ...'

Varney chuckled. 'Despite your rigorous denial of such things, I can see I have piqued your curiosity concerning these matters and it is a most appropriate question to ask Police Constable Colverson.'

'And are you able to answer it?' Abberline wanted to know.

Varney pursed his lips and concentrated. 'Under normal circumstances I would be bound to secrecy, but, as I have already taken you into my confidence on so many matters, I feel I can divulge certain facts on the strict understanding that this information goes no further. Do you swear?'

Colverson nodded. 'Absolutely, Sir Francis.'

'Chief Inspector?'

Abberline paused and then said: 'No-one would believe me anyway.'

'Quite so. Very well. The world knows that His Royal Highness, Prince Albert died on 14th December 1861. What the world does not know, of course, is the existence of the Blood Covenant and all that it implies. Her Majesty, distraught at the thought of losing her dear husband and faithful advisor and companion, sought my advice on a certain matter.

'She wanted to know if you could save his life,' Colverson interjected. 'Like you did the Inspector's.'

'Stop interrupting, Colverson,' Abberline told him.

'Sorry sir.'

'No apologies needed Constable,' Varney said. 'You are, in fact, quite right. Had it been a physical wound I might well have been able to do just that and no-one would have been any the wiser. Unfortunately, the Prince Regent's condition was too far advanced and only one solution presented itself. To prolong the Prince's existence I would have to turn him into a full-fledged member of my own fraternity. In short, a vampire. To the world it would seem like a miraculous recovery but there was always the risk that his true nature may be revealed. Servants are such gossips, you know and then there was the problem of providing a continuous supply of Nancy's. No, no, that would not do at all and so we devised an alternative scheme. Her Majesty's love for her husband was such that she would pay any price not to lose him, even if that meant living apart for most of the time and playing the part of a lifelong grieving widow. To do anything else would invite unsavoury advances from impoverished foreign royalty and that could not be countenanced. And so, at Her Majesty's bidding I turned Prince Albert. As the nation mourned, the Prince was spirited away to live a life of solitude and seclusion. I arranged for our most discrete Nancy's to pay regular visits and, when royal duties allow, Her Majesty and Prince Albert meet clandestinely. Fortunately, today was one such occasion.'

'Incredible,' Abberline murmured.

'Incredible? No. Simply the power of love, Chief Inspector. Does that alter your perception at all?'

Abberline thought for a while and then said: 'When all logical and rational thought processes fail to provide a definitive answer, and lacking any empirical evidence to the contrary, it is incumbent upon the detective mind to consider a less empirical solution.'

'Bravo, Chief Inspector. I do believe we will make a convert of you yet.'

*

As their journey neared its end, Varney outlined his plan for neutralising the threat posed by Ferenc Nadasdy.

'It is really quite simple. Nadasdy will come for me, of that there is no doubt. I believe it will be soon. He intended perhaps to end this affair the other night but was interrupted by your presence. I have therefore sent all the girls to other establishments under Rawshank's protection whilst I await

Nadasdy's coming at Sanguine House like a good little fly caught in a web of my own devising.'

'And should he oblige you in this regard?'

'We will fight, naturally. That is the only way it can end after all this time.'

'And you intend to kill him?'

'I most assuredly do.'

'I am afraid cold blooded murder doesn't sit well with me, Sir Francis.'

'After he has killed five innocent women would you not happily send him to the gallows yourself?'

'As part of the legal justice system, yes, although I take no pleasure in ending a life, however tainted it might be.'

'My aplogies, Chief Inspector. I misspoke. It is a fine distinction I admit, but, under the circumstances, I fail to see the difference. The outcome is the same, surely?'

'You claim that Ferenc Nadasdy is responsible for these Ripper murders, correct?'

'Undoubtedly.'

'And what of the guise that Nadasdy now inhabits? Does he not deserve some consideration? Some justice other than summary execution for being forced to commit crimes against his will?'

'Your compassion does you credit Chief Inspector, but, if it will salve your conscience, let me say this: Ferenc Nadasdy has been searching for over 200 years to find a soul as black and as corrupt as his own that would allow him this much control. He has been able to exert malign influence to be sure, but never to this extent. Whoever this individual is, he is steeped in evil and requires no mercy. The fact is that he ceased to exist the moment Ferenc Nadasdy possessed him and is already well and truly dead.'

'Do you have proof of that?'

Varney threw up his hands in exasperation. 'Proof!? No, I have no empirical proof that you could present to a judge, but you have been commanded by your sovereign to allow me full sway in these matters. Are you intending to disobey a royal command, Chief Inspector?'

'Not at all,' said Abberline calmly. 'What I am going to do is follow the letter of the law. In all matters concerning Ferenc Nadasdy I will bow to your authority. In the meantime, I will busy myself with tracking down and arresting Jack the Ripper whoever he may be.'

'But they are one and the same!'

'Perhaps. And if you can present me with irrefutable proof of that ...'

'Proof! Proof! Always proof!'

For long seconds, Varney studied Abberline's face as if seeking the answer to some inexplicable riddle in the lines and contours he found there. With a small nod of his head, as though he had attained whatever enlightenment he sought, he began to speak.

'Very well Chief Inspector, there may be a way to give you your proof. You will admit that the man known as Frank Nasty is now your prime suspect, yes?'

'Yes.'

'Good. Then I suggest you find him, Chief Inspector before he finds me. If you do, perhaps you will do be the honour of simply keeping him under close surveillance and only intervene if he attempts to commit a crime of any sort, does that sound reasonable?'

'So far, but where does your burden of proof come in?'

'I am coming to that. Having identified him, I ask that you search his dwelling, his place of work, anywhere he frequents or is liable to secrete something he holds most precious. If you do that, I believe you will find the hiding place of the skull of Ferenc Nadasdy. If you can obtain it, I would be obliged if you would destroy it immediately. If you do, there is a chance, slim at best but a chance nonetheless, that doing so will sever Nadasdy's hold on this realm and release the individual he inhabits forthwith. You may then deal as you wish with the husk that remains, if indeed he still lives. Granted this will present you with a rather complicated dilemma, but I believe it will both prove my point and prevent me from having to engage personally in any unpleasantness. Does that appear equitable, Chief Inspector?'

'What if destroying the skull has no effect on the murderous intentions of Frank Nasty?'

'Then it would appear that I was mistaken in that respect. That is a risk we both must take. Are you a gambling man, Chief Inspector?'

'Not when lives are at stake.'

'Then I fear you may have to break the habit of a lifetime in this one instance. Are we in agreement?'

'What other choice do I have?'

'None.'

'Then we are in agreement.'

'Splendid. Now, shall I drop you off at the station or shall we toast our accord with a nice pot of tea and a slice of fruit cake at a little coffee shop I know?'

*

''Course. As an artist you'd have a finer appreciation of the undraped female form, isn't that right?'

Clive Mortimer swallowed loudly. 'I ...err ...I usually paint pictures of family groups. Or pets. Yes, I do a lot of pets.'

'So, a ripe, female figure like wot I possess would be a challenge you might say? I mean, I wouldn't mind if a fine gentleman like yourself were to run his eyes over every single inch of my undraped flesh. Just to get the details right, of course.'

'Undraped, you say?'

'Every inch. Bare as a babe.'

Colverson rapped on the table with his night stick. 'Enough of your shenanigans, Lily May,' he said. 'You're here to give a description of the man you saw running out of the house when Emma was murdered.'

Lily May pouted. 'Spoilsport,' she said. 'I was only having a bit of fun.'

'Nothing about murder is fun, Lily May. 'And you ...' he pointed his night stick at Mortimer. 'You keep your mind on the job in hand and less on undraped forms. How can you expect to capture a true likeness if your mind is elsewhere and your hand is shaking?'

Mortimer nodded. 'Of course. Yes. Now, Miss, what about his eyes?'

'Yes.'

'Yes?'

'Yes, he definitely had eyes.'

Colverson groaned and moved away. Abberline called him to one side. 'How is our artist progressing?' he asked.

'In fits and starts. He's never been surrounded by so many attractive women in his life and I doubt if any of them got a real look at the culprit anyway.'

'I tend to agree, but it pays to be thorough. It's just possible they may have noticed something that we missed, but the final draft will depend on our own observation and that of Sir Francis and Mr. Rawshank I'm sure. After that, we can distribute it to all our men with instructions to be on the lookout.'

'Do you really think this plan of Sir Francis is going to work, sir?'

'It has its merits, but time is against us. Sir Francis is convinced that this Nadasdy character will make another attempt on his life and we have been ordered by the highest authority in the land to let Sir Francis have his way in this matter.'

'It goes against the grain, sir. Especially as we're not allowed to tell our own men the true nature of this enterprise.'

'I couldn't agree more, which is why we will be keeping a discrete watch on Sanguine House in case of mishaps. If we can use this sketch to locate Nadasdy beforehand we can, at least, forewarn Sir Francis of his movements.'

*

They found the priest in the church. On his knees. Praying. A common enough occurrence you might think, but there was something about the man's aspect, the fevered tone of his voice, that betokened a troubled soul rather than someone at peace with his calling and finding comfort from his commune with his Lord and saviour. Abberline waited patiently for a natural break in this one-sided dialogue. Finding none, he offered a discrete cough by way on introduction. Father Cheshire leapt to his feet as though galvanised, turning swiftly and clutching the heavy crucifix that he wore around his neck.

'My apologies, Father,' Abberline said. 'I did not mean to

startle you. My name is Detective Chief Inspector Abberline. I believe you have already met Constable Colverson.'

Father Cheshire blinked like an owl newly introduced to sunlight and then collected himself.

'Yes, yes. Constable Colverson. We met at the station. You were kind enough to take my statement.'

'That's right, sir. That's why we're here.'

'Really? Has there been some development?'

'You could say that.' Abberline took an artist's impression from his pocket and passed it to Father Cheshire. 'Do you recognise this man, Father?'

Father Cheshire studied the drawing for long seconds. 'Yes,' he said finally. 'Yes, this is the man I encountered at Sanguine House. Have you found him?'

'Not yet, but we are looking for him.'

'Then you believe me?' A light of hope shone in Father Cheshire's eyes.

'We have reason to believe that he is a dangerous individual who could be responsible for several deaths,' Abberline said cautiously. 'If this is the man you encountered it may be that he is seeking to eliminate anyone who could incriminate him. We came to warn you to be careful, Father, until he is apprehended.'

'Have no fear, Chief Inspector. My faith will protect me.'

'I'm sure it will, but perhaps a long overdue visit to a seminary somewhere quiet and peaceful might be in order? Just for a week or so, say?'

'I wouldn't dream of abandoning my flock, Chief Inspector.'

'A noble aspiration, Father, but even the most vigilant of shepherds cannot always save his flock from the predations of a rabid wolf and may even fall victim himself if he is not careful.'

'I thank you for your concern, Chief Inspector and may the Good Lord smile upon your endeavours, but I take my guidance from the Good Book. Therein I believe I will receive all the help and guidance I require.'

'As you will, Father, but please, take no unnecessary risks until we have this felon under lock and key.'

'I shall pray for your success, Chief Inspector.'

'Most kind. Well, we must be about our business. Keep the likeness, Father. Should you happen to see him, please do not approach him. Find the nearest policeman and report the sighting. We will handle things from there. Good day, Father.'

'God bless you my son.'

Father Cheshire watched them leave with a martyrs smile upon his face. These good men may indeed find success, but it will take more than mortal efforts to wipe this evil from the face of the earth of that he was sure. The Holy Bible had indeed provided comfort and guidance and Father Cheshire was convinced that only he knew the true way to put an end to this devil's spawn. It would call for a sacrifice of mighty proportions but it was God's will and as his chosen emissary, Father Cheshire was more than willing to make that sacrifice.

*

Every constable on the beat was given the artist's sketch of the man known as Frank Nasty. They had strict instructions to scour the streets, to ask as many people as possible if they recognised him, but, if spotted, under no circumstances were they to confront him. Identify, follow and report back when they were able with his exact location.

It was a constable named Tebbitt who made the breakthrough. Even then it was only because of a crowd outside a barber shop, Chapman's in Southwick Street. Aside from the oddity of such a gathering there was nothing suspicious about their behaviour, but Tebbitt decided to make enquiries anyway.

'We're waiting for a haircut,' he was told.

Tebbitt glanced at the shop door. 'It says "closed",' he said.

'I know that,' his informant said. 'Bugger's been closed for three days now. No-one knows where he's gone.'

'And yet, you're still waiting?'

'What else are we supposed to do?'

Tebbitt pulled the sketch from his pocket. 'Do you know this man?' he asked.

'That's him! George Chapman. This is his shop!'

Once Tebbitt had relayed this information to Whitechapel, Abberline and Colverson made haste to continue their enquiries. The true nature of their mission was too delicate to entrust to other hands, and so, they formed a two man search party. A cursory search of the borough records revealed that the premises had been leased in the name of Seweryn Antonowicz Klosowski. It also listed his home address.

'Chapman was the name of the previous tenant,' Abberline said as they made their way towards the barber shop. 'Klosowski has only been in this country a few months from his native Poland. He took over the shop and the name.'

'Trying to blend in, you think, sir?' Colverson asked.

'Quite possibly. He has a strong accent and mediocre barbering skills, but it gave him a start.'

'Does he live above the shop?'

'No. He has rooms in Leadwell Street. Lives there with his wife, one Lucie Badewski apparently. If the shop proves futile, that will be our next port of call.'

In order to avoid undue attention, the two policemen entered through a badly secured back door. The shop was dingy and damp. It took hardly any time at all to investigate its contents. The usual barbering equipment, scissors, razors etc. which could have been murder weapons were secured in a large satchel for later examination. The upstairs rooms were empty save for broken furniture. Wall panels were knocked and loose floorboards torn up to disclose any potential hiding place big enough for a skull.

Nothing of the sort presented itself.

'Waste of time, sir,' Colverson concluded.

'I agree. Let's move on and see if we can discover anything on his home ground.'

*

421 Leadwell Street was one of many anonymous, run-down dwellings that besmirched that part of the metropolis with their unrepentant air of decay. The Chapman's lived in two rooms on the ground floor back. A tiny woman with haunted eyes and a nervous demeanour opened the door a bare inch and peered out in response to Abberline's knock.

'Yes?' she enquired in a thick Polish accent.

'My name is Detective Chief Inspector Abberline and this is Constable Colverson. Do I have the pleasure of addressing Lucie Badewski?'

The woman blinked as though the question was too difficult for an instant response and required considerable thought. 'Yes,' she finally admitted. 'But I do nothing wrong. Police go away.'

She made to close the door but Colverson's trusty Betsy had insinuated itself between the door and the jamb in an effort to prolong the conversation. The woman glared at it balefully. 'Hey!' she said. 'You no do. You go away.'

'Forgive me, madam,' Abberline smiled. 'We have urgent

business with your husband, George Chapman. Is he here by any chance?'

A sly gleam entered the woman's eye. 'George? No, he not here. He away on business.'

'Business? Would that be barbering business? A trifle unusual, wouldn't you say when he has a perfectly good barber shop just three streets away?'

The woman shrugged.

'Perhaps we could come in anyway. I have a warrant you see, signed by a judge, which gives me the authority to search these premises for certain items pertaining to a current investigation. May we come in and do just that?'

How much the woman understood of what had just been said would forever remain a mystery as would the existence of such a warrant without concrete evidence to justify it, but needs must when the devil drives. The woman gave a small nod of submission and opened the door.

Once inside, Lucie Badewski limped to a dilapidated wooden chair, wincing as she lowered herself gingerly onto it. She wasn't an old woman, not more than thirty Abberline guessed, but she moved like one, indicating some injury or ailment. Her eyes were dark-ringed and sunken, her skin creased with worry and fatigue. She appeared nervous and ill at ease. Abberline had seen all these signs before. Women whose husbands ruled with a heavy hand and a wide leather belt. If he proved guilty of nothing else, Abberline was seized with a desire to bring George Chapman to justice for this crime alone.

'Are you quite well?' he asked. 'Only you seem in pain.'

'I am ...' she stumbled over the word, pronouncing it clearly and emphatically. '...oh-kay.'

'There are doctors, free hospitals. I can give you the address.'

'No doctors!' Her voice was almost a shout. A reaction Abberline was also familiar with. No doctors. No outsiders.

However bad the pain, it would be far worse if the victim dared to parade their condition to a stranger.

'Very well,' Abberline said. 'With your permission we will begin our search. We will try not to disturb anything too much.'

The woman gave a harsh laugh. 'What there to disturb?'

Abberline had to admit that she had a point. A rickety table, two chairs with broken legs, a stove and some rudimentary cooking utensils. In the next room, a broken-down bed, a small dresser and a wardrobe with one door missing containing some threadbare items of male and female clothing. Nowhere to hide a skull. Once again walls were rapped and loose floorboards pried up revealing nothing.

'What you look for?' Lucie asked.

'A smallish item, roughly the size of a teapot,' Abberline told her.

'And you think George has this "teapot"?'

'We think he might. Is there anywhere else he might have hidden such an item?'

She shrugged. 'He never tell me his business.'

'But he goes on many business trips, does he?'

'Sometimes.'

'Do you know where he goes?'

'He never say. But he been gone a long time this time. I think maybe he not come back this time. You think he might not?'

Abberline couldn't fail to notice the gleam of hope in the woman's eyes.

'I think it might be best if you consider other arrangements. Just in case he does not,' he said.

The woman nodded. 'I do that,' she said.

*

'And there is no sign of the skull?' Varney asked.

'None whatsoever,' Abberline told him.

'He has no other properties or access to a bank that might hold precious items for him?'

'None that we can find. Nor any affiliations or close associates. He is a loner who keeps to himself.'

'A wise move to disguise his true intentions.'

'Quite possibly. But that does not mean that he is a possessed soul, simply a mentally disturbed killer who needs to be brought to justice.'

Varney sighed. 'You exasperate me, Chief Inspector, you really do.'

'The feeling is mutual, Sir Francis.'

Varney roared with laughter. 'My word but you make for an implacable adversary my dear Chief Inspector. I feel sorry for any quarry you set your sights on.'

'I take that as a compliment.'

'As you should. But you know where this leaves us.'

'If we cannot trace the man, we must assume that he will break cover to come to Sanguine House to confront you in person.'

'Exactly. And I would remind you of Her Majesty's instructions concerning such a confrontation.'

'I haven't forgotten, but it is my duty to safeguard the public at all costs, and that includes you Sir Francis.'

'What would you suggest?'

'A round the clock guard around Sanguine House, ready to move in when Nadasdy shows his face.'

Varney shook his head. 'Too obvious.'

'Plain clothes officers only.'

'Still too obvious.'

Now it was Abberline's turn to sigh. 'Very well. Regular patrols during the day to reduce the possibility of any unwanted visitors and, at night, which would seem the most likely time for an incursion, just myself and Constable

Colverson.'

'At a discrete distance and only to interfere if my own efforts prove futile?'

'As you wish.'

'Then we are in accord once again Chief Inspector, and you have my thanks for your concern over my safety.'

'Then until tonight, Sir Francis. Until tonight.'

*

Frank Nasty knew he could not go back to 421 Leadwell Street. Not yet anyway. Lucie would keep the skull hidden if she knew what was good for her. He would retrieve it when his mission was over. **His** mission? No, not his, the skull's mission. It spoke to him inside his head. Filled him with delicious ideas and images of violence. Not that he was any stranger to violence. Nor to killing. He'd lost count of how many whores he'd topped all over the world before the skull had come into his life. That's why he'd had to keep moving. Always one step ahead of the police. It was a strategy that had worked well for him. After this was over he had his sights set on America. Plenty of rich pickings there. Part of him hoped the skull's voice would leave him be once he had finished his dirty work. But part of him hoped it would not. These latest kills had been special. The cutting, the blood, the taste, the smell of it was all so ... unworldly. He'd won the skull in a card game with a German seaman. From the second the skull had been placed on the table to cover the German's bet it had spoken to him. Not in words. Emotions, feelings, love, hate, desire for revenge flooding into him like molten lava. He knew he had to have it. To be more precise, he knew that the skull had to have him. He was tempted to return to his lodgings and retrieve it now so that he could hold it close, keep it with him, but that would be foolish. He needed it safe should the unthinkable happen to him / them. He wasn't sure anymore if he was one person or two. He only knew that the end of the skull's mission was in sight and when it was finished he would be re-united with the skull. And then what adventures they would have!

In the meantime, he would have to lay low until the time was right. Finding a hiding place was not too difficult. Rose Mylett was not the first woman he had been unfaithful with, not by a long chalk. Lucie knew, she had to, he had never kept it a secret, but she never complained. Not more than once anyway, and whilst she was healing he was free to take his pleasure with whomever he pleased.

Rose Mylett. Twenty-six years old, curly chestnut hair, a heart shaped face, fair skin and dark eyes. A seamstress by trade. She had comfortable rooms in a boarding house with a landlady who turned a blind eye to her charges comings and goings for a small remittance. Rose Mylett who thought he loved her and would soon leave his wife so they could set up home together. She never stopped talking about it in fact, going on and on about what a wonderful life they would have together. That had been her undoing in the end. He just had to stop her talking. Rose Mylett who knew nothing of the ways of the world and now never would. She lay now on the bed, stark naked save for a red scarf wrapped around her throat. The scarf that he had pulled so tight that it choked off her breath, made her eyes bulge from their sockets, made her face purple and her tongue protrude. Tighter and tighter he had pulled until the choking, gurgling noises ceased and her limbs stopped thrashing. He'd been inside her at the time and the thrashing excited him more than their usual coupling however robust that may have been. After she lay still he had continued his enjoyment until her flesh began to cool. Then he had gotten dressed. He had not used his blade upon her. No. That particular delight was reserved for special victims. Those that served Varney who was, himself, not long for this world. By this time tomorrow his task would be complete and Varney would be no more. He kissed Rose Mylett one last time upon the lips and made his way out into the night.

*

Night brought fog. Not the pea souper for which London was notorious, but a chilly, grey miasma that wafted over the water and enclosed man, beast and masonry with a damp embrace.

Abberline and Colverson, dressed as rough labourers, muffled against the cold, lurked in an alley opposite Sanguine House. The same shadows and swirling fingers of fog that kept them hidden so successfully also all but obscured their view of Varney's bolt hole.

'Damn the man,' Abberline muttered. 'If he'd let us deploy a squad of men this would be much easier.'

Colverson rubbed his arms with his gloved hands in an effort to keep out the chill. This was their third night in a row keeping vigil and it looked like it was going to be a long one. 'Do you really think he'll show up, sir?' he asked.

'The man seems to have disappeared into thin air, so this is our best hope,' Abberline responded.

'At least there's been no more killings.'

'Thank Heaven for small mercies.'

'Maybe we frightened him off the last time. With all the enquiries we've been making, he could have packed up and moved on.'

'Whatever he may be, man or monster, he is determined above all else and fixated upon Sir Francis moreover. He'll turn up, Colverson, you mark my words.'

Further down the street, another figure, cloaked in clerical black, a large leather valise at his feet, shivered against the night. However pleased he had been to hear that the police were now taking his complaint seriously, he had no hope that they would succeed. This was an entity so far beyond their abilities and comprehension that their best efforts would be for nought. Only he knew how to snuff this evil out of existence. It was not something the police would countenance. It was something only a disciple of the Lord could do. He had his equipment with him. He had his faith. All he needed now was to find his prey. This place, this den of iniquity, had been the scene of their first encounter. There were other such establishments, it's true, but something drew Father Cheshire back to this location. The very walls and beams of the place reeked of dissolution. And licentiousness. He could almost smell the reek of evil emanating from its walls. His prey would return here eventually, of that he was sure. When he did, Father Cheshire would be waiting. And then, if his nerve did not fail him, he would put an end to him once and for all, even if it cost him his life.

*

Abberline watched a dim glow move from room to room before settling in the downstairs drawing room. Varney doing his rounds. Not to make sure that the house was secure from intruders, oh, no, just the opposite.

'What point baiting a trap if it is too difficult for the prey to enter it?' he had argued.

He had a point, but Abberline was not happy about it. Allowing a madman free access to a potential victim went very much against the grain. Lord knows what the Commissioner would say if – when – he found out. Endangering the life of a peer of the realm for reasons that could not be disclosed could be a career ending proposition. Varney had given Abberline the freedom to withdraw from the fray completely, then, whatever happened could not be laid at his door. Abberline knew that wasn't really true. Should Varney be killed and the perpetrator linked to the Ripper murders, which was extremely possible, then the blame would be laid firmly at Abberline's door despite Varney's assurances otherwise.

It was as he was mulling over this unfortunate state of affairs that he saw movement. Just a shadow among shadows, dancing in and out of the swirling fog to a tune that only they could hear.

Abberline nudged Colverson. 'There!' he hissed. 'Across the street. Do you see?'

'Where?' Colverson whispered back. 'With this blessed fog I can barely see my hand in front of my face.'

'My eyesight appears to have improved of late,' Abberline muttered. 'Maybe Mrs. Abberline is using more carrots in her mutton stew.'

'Or it could be, you know, the transfusion Sir Francis gave you. He said it would improve your vigour. Maybe it improves your senses too.'

'That's one maybe too many for my liking. Look, there, do you see him now?'

'I don't ...wait, yes, I see it. Is it him do you think?'

'Could be. Too dark to be sure even with my improved eyesight. We shall just have to wait and see what transpires.'

As they watched, the dark shape moved towards the front door of Sanguine House, paused for a second, tried the handle, pushed the door open and disappeared inside.

'He's going in the front door!' Abberline hissed. 'The nerve of the man!'

'Shall we move in now, sir?'

'Not yet. Sir Francis was very clear on that point. We are only to intervene in the event of a dire emergency.'

'But how are we to know if it's an emergency if we can't see what's going on?'

'We'll give it five minutes. If one or the other of them has not appeared by then, we move in quietly and try to see what's going on inside. Until then we stay put.'

The two policemen may have been immobilised by duty, but God's chosen one was not bound by any such constrictions. As the shadowy figure entered Sanguine House, Father Cheshire also made his move. Abberline and Colverson were so focused on the front of the house that they failed to notice a second figure slip from concealment and make its way down the side of the house to the same back door that had given him access on his previous visit. Now, as then, his intrusion must be clandestine. It would not do to alert the house's occupants to his presence until he was ready. By then it would be far too late for any of them to escape their fate.

*

Houses are never truly quiet. A gurgle in the pipes. The creak of timbers. The squeak of a badly hung door. A loose coal toppling in the sooty fireplace. The rustle of a window pane when the wind blows. A whole symphony of sounds. Houses live. They breathe, they are never still. Not even on a night like this when Sanguine House could be forgiven for holding its breath, cocooned as it was in an overcoat of enveloping fog isolating it from any outside disturbances.

Varney knew Sanguine House well. Knew its every nook and cranny, its every breath, its every sigh and groan. Nothing and no-one could intrude on the nocturnal whispers that had imprinted themselves upon his mind. Even so, he was mildly surprised to see a dark figure standing in the doorway to the drawing room where he sat, a single lamp casting an uncertain glow upon his features, the ceremonial claymore lying across his lap, its edge as sharp now as it had been all those years ago when he had used it to cleave Ferenc Nadasdy's head from his shoulders.

'Do come in,' Varney said, politely. 'No need to stand on ceremony.'

The man known colloquially as Frank Nasty took a pace forward. The pale lantern light painted his face in dark shadows and ugly angles, lending his eyes a baleful glare.

An ugly brute to be sure, but only in the eyes did Varney glimpse the remnants of the Ferenc Nadasdy he had known. Abberline had been right in one respect. Whatever motivated this carapace of flesh and bone, this was not wholly Ferenc Nadasdy. If Varney allowed himself to think that, then the thought of the power needed to animate this fleshy puppet after so many years may prove his undoing. No, better to regard him as Frank Nasty, a shadow of someone, some thing, that had once been a man and a threat to empire. It had been Varney's duty then to defend that empire by disposing of the threat as it was his duty now to write finis to that particular chapter of history. Or die trying.

'Would you care for some refreshment before we begin, Frank? I may call you Frank, may'nt I? George seems so plebeian and Ferenc ... well, we never were on first name terms were we? And I see only a pale glimmer of that person here, so Frank it shall be.'

Nasty's only reply was an animal growl. A rage simmering and building for over two hundred years rendering him speechless now that the moment of his triumph seemed within reach. This man had taken everything from him, not least of which was his corporeal life and he had repaid him in kind by slaughtering those women who meant so much to him. It was a just and fitting punishment that he should suffer thus before the final act of this drama was played out.

'I don't suppose you've been able to keep up with the latest news these last few hundred years have you?' Varney asked. 'Why not sit down and take a glass of brandy whilst I bring you up to date.'

Nasty said nothing, his lip simply curled away from his teeth in a death's head grimace.

'No?' Varney said. 'As you wish. I just thought you might like to know what happened to Elizabeth, that's all.'

Nasty's body tensed, his hands clenching and unclenching convulsively. 'You are not fit to speak her name!' Nasty roared.

Varney clasped a hand to his chest in mock indignation. Elizabeth Bathory had been Ferenc Nadasdy's weakness all those years ago. His love had made him careless and maybe, just maybe, she could do the same thing now, giving Varney some small advantage once more. 'I?' he said. 'I did nothing to harm your wife. I may have caused her a little embarrassment. That business with the wagon wheel. Rawshank's idea if I'm honest. I didn't entirely approve, but then, she was a lovely woman.'

Nasty growled, deep in his throat and took a half step forward, tensing to spring.

'She survived you know,' Varney told him and Nasty paused, his curiosity piqued. Varney smiled inwardly as he continued. 'I thought you'd like to know that. She lived quite a while, but it can't have been very pleasant for her. The villagers took charge of her welfare and, well, you know how she treated them, the tortures she inflicted upon them for no other reason than it amused her. They kept her confined in one room of the castle and fed her enough to keep her alive and healthy enough to withstand the many and inventive ways they devised to torment her. Many of which she invented herself. You know the sort of thing. Needles under the fingernails, the occasional flogging for minor infractions, scaldings, being made to walk barefoot on broken glass. I believe at one point they pulled out all her teeth, and, oh, yes, my favourite. Every year at the local cattle auction, she was paraded naked through the streets and sold off for one night to the highest bidder to do with as he wished. They sold tickets of course because people do so love to watch.'

The dam of emotion inside Frank Nasty broke under Varney's goading. With an animal roar he sprang forward, hands reaching for Varney's throat, but Varney was too quick. Springing to his feet, he swung the mighty claymore, hoping to replicate in one movement the same feat he had performed centuries past. In that he was mistaken. The blow was a mighty one and, had it been full-square on target would have had the desired effect, but Nasty's forward lunge spoiled Varney's aim by a fraction. Instead of striking at the neck and neatly severing head from torso, the claymore struck the side of Nasty's head. The blow severed an ear and tore a chunk of flesh from his face even as it sent him crashing to the floor. Even so, Varney had every hope that the wound would be enough to incapacitate his foe leaving him vulnerable for the killing stroke. In that too, he would be disappointed. Nasty rolled with the blow and came onto his knees, blood streaming down his face. Even as Varney raised the claymore once more, Nasty reached inside his coat, producing a wicked looking carving knife and sprang forward. In that moment, Varney realised his error in his choice of weapon. On the field of battle, the claymore is a mighty weapon but in cramped, confined quarters its weight and size proved a hindrance.

Nasty ducked beneath Varney's swing, slashing with his knife and drawing blood, the force of his charge slamming Varney backwards, smashing into the table where the room's sole source of illumination rested. The table shattered, the lamp falling to the floor, plunging the room into darkness.

*

On the upstairs landing of Sanguine House, Father Peter Cheshire went about God's work. He heard the sound of voices from below but could not distinguish the words. The rest of the house seemed deserted and for that he was thankful. Panderers to evil and slaves of Satan they may have been but it still pricked his conscience that his plan may have caused the deaths of those who may yet be able to seek redemption. Why his quarry would seek out an almost empty dwelling was a mystery. Maybe that was the cause of the raised voices from below. Maybe he expected to find more nymphs of darkness upon which he could slake his unearthly appetites. It mattered not. Father Cheshire retrieved the bottles of oil from his valise and spread the contents liberally along the upstairs carpets and walls. He then proceeded to make his way downstairs performing the same anointment. One bottle he made sure to save. That one was for his use alone. The sounds from below had erupted from raised voices to the unmistakable sound of violence. So be it. A distraction may make his job easier. Father Cheshire began to hum a favourite hymn softly. He was a man who was resigned to his fate and therefore happy in his work.

*

Across the street, two of Scotland Yard's finest did not have even Father Cheshire's slight insight into the events taking place inside Sanguine House. They only knew that the single light that had shed a dim glow in the downstairs window had suddenly been extinguished.

'Damn it!' Abberline said. 'What the hell does that mean?'

Colverson had no informed response. 'Should I sneak over for a peek in the window, sir?' he asked.

'Our orders are to wait until one or the other emerges. Backed by a royal command no less. We wait, Colverson. For now at least.

*

The absence of light proved no great handicap for the two combatants since their natural abilities allowed them to see almost as well in the dark as during the brightest day.

Scrambling to his feet, Varney kicked Nasty's fallen knife across the room and snatched up an elegant ebony cane, abandoning the heavier, clumsier, claymore that had mistakenly been his weapon of choice. The slash across his stomach was bleeding but not very much, and it would be a reminder to be more careful from now on. With a twist of the cane's handle, the outer casing fell away to reveal a slim, but deadly, blade. It didn't have the power of the claymore, but it had a longer reach than Nasty's knife. As Nasty rose up from the wreckage of the demolished table, Varney exercised this advantage by opening a long gash across Nasty's upper arm eliciting a howl of pain.

Undeterred, Nasty snatched up a sturdy, straight backed chair and hurled it with enough force to make Varney throw up his left arm to protect himself. Momentarily off-balance and unsighted, Varney barely had time to see Nasty closing upon him, his hands outstretched for Varney's throat, the butcher's knife lost and forgotten in the debris of smashed furniture, his fury overriding his senses like a tidal wave. Varney barely had time to raise his sword, but it was enough. Nasty's own momentum impaled him on the sword's tip and such was the power of his movement that he forced the blade fully through his body until his hands closed around Varney's throat. Nor did his headlong charge end there. Roaring like a wounded beast, Nasty threw them back, bursting through the doors of the drawing room to crash, sprawling onto the hall floor. Nasty's hold was like iron around Varney's throat, squeezing the air from his lungs. Varney kicked and writhed, his hands raking Nasty's face, digging deep into the socket of his left eye, rupturing the soft flesh he found there and ripping the orb from its socket. Apart from a renewed howl of agony, this did not have the expected result and Nasty's grip, if anything, intensified. Varney's last thought before a wave of blackness engulfed him was that he would never again make the mistake of underestimating an opponent.

As Varney's form became limp, Nasty finally released his grip. As his rage slowly began to subside to be replaced by wave upon wave of sickening pain, he stumbled to his feet, gripping the hilt of the sword that still pierced his body and, with deep grunts of agony, slowly pulled it free from his flesh to deposit it upon Varney's prone form. He stood there, bent double, panting, blood and gore dripping from his mutilated eye socket and the open wound which lacerated the side of his face. His strength was ebbing, but that didn't matter. He still had enough strength to make sure his enemy was finally dead and after that his own fate was immaterial. It occurred to him that it would be justice of a most poetic kind to use the very instrument that had ended his own life to put an end to Varney once and for all. As he turned to shuffle back to the dining room to retrieve the claymore he noticed a still, silent, figure standing at the bottom of the staircase. He could not discern the features clearly, but the voice, when the figure spoke, was vaguely reminiscent.

'In the name of the Lord God, I banish thee from this realm forevermore.'

It was then that Nasty remembered. The loathsome priest who had interrupted his first attempt at confronting Varney. His presence here at this time was a mystery but not one that Nasty had time to unravel. There was a spark of light. A match flared, was dropped like a miniature comet in the night sky and then the priest exploded in a column of flame. He screamed as the fire engulfed him, travelling with uncanny speed up the stairs and across the landing. And then the priest of living fire moved forward.

*

Across the street, Abberline and Colverson saw flickers of light appear through the drawing room window. It was a sight that Abberline would, most definitely, classify as a dire emergency.

'Run, Colverson, run!' Abberline shouted and both men charged across the street bursting through the front door and stepping into the jaws of hell.

The fire was spreading with rapacious appetite consuming carpets, doors and bannisters. In the centre of the inferno, two figures, entwined like lovers in a macabre dance whirled and swayed.

Smoke stung their eyes and heat burned their lungs. At first, Abberline feared that one of the flaming figures was Varney but Colverson grabbed his arm.

'There, sir!' he coughed, pointing to a still figure lying on the floor, about to be engulfed by the rapidly spreading pool of flame.

With no further word spoken, Abberline and Colverson grabbed Varney under the arms and dragged him from the burning building into the cool, damp, London night. Behind them, dimly visible in the smoke and the flames, the two figures continued their torrid waltz until a final misstep caused them to come crashing to the floor. As the flames roared their fury into the night the two bodies were obscured from view, still entwined but now surrendered to whatever fate may await them.

*

Sanguine House could not be saved. By some miracle, the houses on either side were only slightly damaged and the death count that night was confined to two. One was identified as Father Peter Cheshire thanks largely to a letter he had left in the church detailing his proposed activities. The other was formally identified by Sir Francis Varney, whose recovery was as swift as it was unlikely, as George Chapman, formerly known as Seweryn Antonowicz Klosowski, latterly using the pseudonym Frank Nasty. It was formally surmised that his many identities was symptomatic of a disturbed mind and, having visited Sanguine House for criminal purposes and having found it empty save for Varney, took his revenge by setting fire to the establishment. The presence of Father Cheshire was put down to the fact that the priest was passing by when he noticed the conflagration and entered the building, good Samaritan that he was, to rescue any inhabitants he might find there, perishing in the process. He was thus hailed as a local hero for his selflessness. Chapman's role in the Jack the Ripper murders was never revealed lest it arouse suspicion as to his true identity, such was the demand of the Blood Covenant and Abberline was forced to abide by its instructions by royal decree.

Although the Ripper murders went officially unsolved and history would show it as a failure on Abberline's prowess as an investigator, he took solace from the fact that those particular crimes ceased from that night forward. He also received some sort of acknowledgement in the form of a letter on palace notepaper commending him for valour in saving the life of Sir Francis Varney from the murderous intentions of a homicidal madman and pyromaniac. Abberline decided, all in all, it was sufficient. Emma Abberline was delighted with the correspondence and it became one of her most prized possessions.

Abberline and Colverson met once more with Varney some days later when he kept his promise to attend a meeting of Emma's reading group. In Abberline's parlour over tea and biscuits the three men put an end, once and for all, to the Ripper murders.

'A pity the skull could not be found,' Varney said.

'Does it still pose a danger?' Abberline asked.

Varney smiled. 'Am I to take it from your question that you now agree that it was indeed the source of all our misery?'

Abberline returned the smile. 'Only a poor detective would ignore the obvious, however improbable it may seem.'

'Splendid. And in answer to your question, I really don't know. We shall have to wait and see.'

'What will you do now, Sir Francis?' Colverson asked.

'What I have always done,' Varney answered. 'Sanguine House needs to be rebuilt but I have other properties, other interests that enable me to continue my work with the Nancy's.'

'And your other interests of a more royal nature?' Abberline asked.

Varney sighed. 'There is a wind of change blowing through the land, Chief Inspector. Times are changing rapidly. I feel that the Blood Covenant will soon become obsolete which means it is even more important that I continue to bolster the Nancy network to forestall any unfortunate happenings that may call for the Covenant to be re-instated. And you, Chief Inspector?'

'I shall continue as I have always done. Crime is ever present and the forces of law and order will always be needed.'

'I believe that your superiors are none too pleased with your apparent failure to apprehend Jack the Ripper and for that I am truly sorry. I wish it could be otherwise'

'A policeman's lot, Sir Francis, is rarely a happy one.'

'Quite so, Chief Inspector, but I have a feeling that a man of your ability, and you Constable Colverson, will have many successes to come to ameliorate your disappointment in this matter. You also have my heartfelt thanks for the small matter of saving my life. And now I have an important engagement with the ladies of your good wife's reading group and it would not do to keep them waiting.'

*

It took Lucie Badewski no time at all to pack. In truth she had little more than the clothes on her back. There was one other item though, that was most important. The only thing that her husband possessed that could possibly be of value. Foolish English policemen. So polite. So respectful. In her homeland such men on such a mission would have stripped her naked and continued their search even then if she had not disclosed the whereabouts of the object they sought. But not here. Not in London. She played the downtrodden drab full well, George's fists and boots had seen to it there was little deception involved in the performance and they had left her alone. As soon as she was sure that they had gone, she reached up to a hidden pocket beneath her skirt and retrieved that most sacred of objects that had no doubt been the object of their visit. To have given it up would have meant her life if George had returned to find it missing. But George would not return. Not now. Of that she was sure. His absence had been too long this time. He was hiding out. He was good at it. Whatever his plan was it would prove to be his undoing. Her Grandmother's gypsy blood told her that much. Or maybe it was just wishful thinking. Either way Lucie Badewski had had enough. She would go as far away as possible. Once the bruises healed she was not a bad looking woman. She would adopt a new name and find some man to look after her. He did not have to be rich or good looking. A kind man. A steady man. She was not greedy. She would find someone, of that she was sure. But what to do with the skull? Leave it behind maybe? Then, if the police returned they would find it. No, there was a better way.

Abe Weisman's pawn shop gave her a good price for it. He haggled of course, such was his way, but she was a hard negotiator when she needed to be and she needed to be now more than ever. The money would be enough to see her out of London and that was all she needed. Abe Weisman, for his part, was equally pleased. He would happily have paid double for a genuine item such as this. He knew several customers of the esoteric or theatrical persuasion who would pay handsomely for such an item. Its obvious age indicated that it had already passed through several hands before and no doubt would again over the years. For now, he secured it in his safe. Too valuable to put on display, besides which, the very sight of it conjured up base images in his mind and the touch of it made his stomach curdle. That in itself would double the asking price, but for now it was best to keep it securely under lock and key.

PRESENT DAY

26

Winkle sat back and thought dark thoughts. How much of this bollocks could he believe? Seven hundred year old vampires living in an old folk's home? Haunted skulls? Jack the sodding Ripper?

'They never found the skull, you say?' he said at last.

'Unfortunately not. It's possible that Ferenc had allies and followers who spirited it away until such a time as he could find another ideal subject to possess.'

'So this Frank Nasty character could have just been your common or garden psycho and not possessed at all?'

'That is undeniably a possibility. However, the nature of his crimes and the nature of other such atrocities since then and current events would indicate that they are the work of the same person.'

Winkle snorted. 'Try telling that to a judge!'

Varney smiled. 'You remind me so much of Chief Inspector Abberline, Mr. Pilkington. I take that as a sign of encouragement.'

'Don't get your hopes up,' Winkle muttered.

'Then consider this, Mr. Pilkington. Even if only tangentially, we have a common goal. The apprehension of this person dubbed The Slasher by the local press. We know for a fact that all his victims thus far have been Nancy's. It seems plain to me that he is repeating the same pattern as he did in 1888. Punishing me by killing those women most dear to me. When he has had his fun, he will come for me and it will all be over one way or another. If it were only my life at risk, I would not care so much, but if his activities continue however, it may shed unwanted light on our existence, however implausible it may sound to you. In a world where mass communication is just the touch of a button away the results could be catastrophic to our continued peaceful existence. In the past such individuals have been dealt with discretely by people like Chief Inspector Abberline and PC Colverson and their successors. When the twentieth century brought new atrocities in the form of two world wars the old legends about vampires were relegated to mere entertainment. It was therefore felt that the services of those who strove to protect us in the past were no longer needed. Perhaps we were too complacent in that assumption. Perhaps we were wrong to dispense with the Abberline's and Colverson's of this world. That, Mr. Pilkington, is where I believe you can come in.'

Winkle thought for second and then threw back his head and laughed until tears streamed down his cheeks. When he finally had control of himself again he said: 'You want me to be your tame copper?'

'Not the term I would use. A consultant maybe. A freelance operative who has the knowledge and experience to discretely investigate those cases that may impinge upon our liberty. There would, of course, be a retainer that goes with the position.'

'Very generous, but the force doesn't even think I'm up to nicking shoplifters in Sainsbury's any more, plus which, Madame Arcati over there thinks I'm heading for the knacker's yard so I'm not going to be of much use to you for much longer am I?'

Varney smiled his benevolent smile. 'You underestimate your ability Mr. Pilkington, and, as for your health, well, I know this has been a lot to take in but maybe you missed that part where I said anyone who is turned into a vampire is immune from disease.'

Winkle stared at him and said nothing.

27

Alice Porter was not in a good mood. It was supposed to be the holiday of a lifetime so what does that good for nothing husband of hers go and do? Sprains his ankle on the first day showing off to some scrawny Brummie slapper wearing nothing but two tea bags and some dental floss between her legs as she sat by the pool. Phil was so concerned about keeping his gut in he tripped on a sun lounger and went arse over tip, knackering his ankle in the process. Spent the rest of the trip hobbling around on crutches and expecting her to wait on him hand and foot.

To make matters worse, she comes back to an answerphone full of messages from customers who haven't been able to get hold of her. Never should have trusted that dimwit Brenda to run things, she thought. She'd tried to get her on her mobile but the dozy cow wasn't answering. Then, to cap it all, Bernie starts on at her about some weird smell that's coming from her place. Alice's Dungeon was on the top floor over Bernie's Adult Book Store and, as she made her way up the stairs she had to admit that he was not wrong. Something was definitely whiffy. She turned the key in the lock and let herself into the small reception area. Everything looked just as she had left it. The smell was stronger now. If she's been eating sushi up here I'll swing for her, Alice thought.

She pushed open the door that lead to the Dungeon and flicked on the light. The smell was almost unbearable now. Enough to make your eyes water. As she took in the familiar surroundings she knew that something was wrong. For a second she couldn't place what. That dummy wasn't there before was it? What's the stupid bitch gone and done? Stringing up a waxworks in the ceiling harness. Alice took one step forward. Her foot landed in something sticky. There was a puddle on the floor, dried up and tacky. She lifted her foot and looked at the mess clinging to the sole of her shoe. Looked from that to the dummy hanging from the harness. Not a dummy she realised. Recognition kicked in and Alice Porter turned away and vomited before running for the stairs.

28

West Street and East Street veered away from each other like distant relatives at a family reunion who have just remembered why they always hated each other. The land between them was called The Triangle. It was home to student bed-sits, takeaways of all manner of creeds and descriptions, pawn shops of optional spellings, and assorted garages and workshops. The street had been cordoned off, traffic was backed up and onlookers drawn by morbid curiosity or professional interest craned their necks in the hope of seeing something juicy.

DCI Cooper almost made it to the finish line before the crowd spotted him. His DC, Patty Bracewell, a slim young woman with short ginger hair and freckles that made her look about fifteen instead of her actual twenty-six, waved him over and lifted up the regulation tape that sealed off the crime scene. It was that movement that alerted the crowd to his presence. The massed ranks of the press swooped like carrion crow on a mouldering carcass. How the hell did they know anyway? Cooper wondered. Now, as he ducked gratefully under the tape, Angela Munro, a news anchor for the local TV station, noted more for her cleavage than her journalistic integrity, shoved a furry caterpillar under his nose.

'Inspector Cooper, what can you tell us about this attack?' she said.

Cooper looked at Bracewell who gave a wry smile and shrugged. 'Miss Munro,' he said, 'as you can see I've only just arrived on the scene. As soon as there is anything to tell you, we'll issue a statement. And it's Detective Chief

Inspector actually.'

'So the police have no clues as to the perpetrator,' she called after him. 'And it's Ms. Munro actually.'

Cooper flinched but let it pass. 'How the hell did they find out so quickly?' he said.

'Probably got a scanner,' Patty said. 'Or someone tweeted it. It's probably gone viral already'

'Don't you just love technology,' Cooper grunted. 'You never had this problem when coppers blew whistles and used a Tardis to call it in.'

'Have you not had your coffee yet?' she asked.

'How did you guess? What have we got?' Cooper held out his hand and Patty placed some latex gloves and a pair of overshoes in his palm. He always forgot to bring his own and Patty was quick on the uptake when it came to her superior officer's foibles. Cooper leant against the wall and pulled on his overshoes and gloves as Patty read from her notebook.

'Single victim. Female. Mid-twenties I'd say.'

'Who found her?'

'A Mrs. Alice Porter. Rents the space from Bernie's Adult Book Shop. Uses it for bondage and discipline therapy.'

She gestured to the shop front cordoned off by police tape and guarded by two constables. The smeared shop window showed copies of what Cooper would have called "mucky mags" when he was young and promises of much more explicit material inside. 'The victim is upstairs in Alice's Dungeon,' Bracewell continued.

'Where is she now?' Cooper asked.

'In the squad car. Harris is with her. She's pretty shaken up.'

'She would be. Get her down to the station, I'll take her statement myself. Right, let's see what we've got.'

Inside, white suited forensics officers roamed like lonely ghosts waiting for the okay to perform their miracles. 'Upstairs, Boss,' Patty told him. 'First door on the left. And Boss, just to let you know, it's a messy one'

'Aren't they all?'

As Cooper stepped inside the first thing to hit him was the smell. A hot, coppery scent that stung the back of his throat. Like a bloodhound on the scent, he followed the smell to a rubber tiled room festooned with shackles whips, gags and other items he didn't recognise and didn't want to. It was also decorated in the blood-red blooms of arterial spray.

'Bloody hell!' Cooper muttered.

The Divisional Surgeon was already there, a bluff Scotsman called MacIntyre. He nodded a greeting.

'What have we got, Mac?' Cooper asked.

'Caucasian female, early twenties, been dead a good while. Weeks rather than days, I'd say.'

'Before the others?'

'You're thinking the same perp?' MacIntyre watched too many TV detective shows. Cooper nodded. 'Certainly a possibility,' MacIntyre said.

'Cause of death?'

'Marks on the throat may indicate strangulation but I doubt it was the cause of death. That's more likely to be blood loss resulting from multiple cuts. I'll know more when I get her back to the lab.'

Patty had told him as much but it was always good to have the details confirmed by an expert. 'You said cuts, not stab wounds?'

'That's right.'

'Thanks, Doc.'

MacIntyre moved away and for a second Cooper was left

alone with the victim. It was the moment he hated most. As if the violation already inflicted upon her wasn't enough, here he was about to commit the act that would sanction obscene poking and prodding. He sighed and forced himself to study the object, he couldn't bring himself to humanise it any more than that at the moment, more carefully. Her arms were stretched above her head, fixed by chains to the ceiling. A gag protruded from her mouth, to muffle the screams presumably, because she would have screamed, of that he was certain. Apart from the gag, she was naked, her body marred by a proliferation of raw cuts criss-crossing the pale flesh that had already started to peel from the bones. The implications were too many to ignore. This was the first victim. Left here to rot whilst the killer went on to commit more atrocities.

'Jesus,' Cooper muttered. He didn't look round but he sensed a presence behind him and knew it would be Patty. 'Any ID?' he asked.

'She had a wallet.' She handed him a plastic evidence bag. Cooper smoothed the plastic so that he could read the name on the driving licence that Patty had made sure was conveniently displayed for his inspection.

'Brenda Dunphy? Name rings a bell.'

'Previous conviction for soliciting,' Patty told him.

Cooper nodded. 'Not surprising. Still, nobody deserves this. All right, let the techies do their job and let's get back to the station. I've a feeling this is going to be a long day.'

29

'It's not sex.' Dirty Alice was adamant about that. 'Not real sex anyway,' she amended. 'You don't even have to take your kit off. Although they do like you to wear something a bit racy. Stockings and suspenders, that sort of thing. And boots. Boots are very popular. The higher the heel the better. The number of times I've sprained my ankle over the years thanks to those ruddy boots. Still, it's better than letting some randy sailor park his tug boat up your hoo-hah any time he feels like it.'

DCI Cooper shuffled the papers in front of him and ran a finger around a suddenly too tight collar. Dirty Alice seemed to have recovered from her shock at finding a mutilated corpse hanging from her ceiling remarkably quickly. Still, in her line of work, shock value is pretty relative. The interview room was suddenly very stuffy. DC Patricia Bracewell, the room's third occupant, stifled a grin. 'Yes, well,' Cooper said. 'If you could just tell us what happened. In your own words.'

Alice settled herself in the uncomfortable plastic chair. 'Well,' she said, 'Phil, that's my husband, common law but who cares these days, he's been promising to take me on a cruise for ages. He had a nice win on the gee-gees a few weeks back and I wanted to take advantage before he pissed the lot up against a wall. But I didn't want to let my regulars down neither. If they can't get their kicks with me they'll bugger off somewhere else. There's no loyalty these days. Not that they'd get the same quality service anywhere else, but some of them don't care. It could be a monkey with a wet dishcloth for all they care. Normally I get our Rosie, that's my youngest, to stand in for me, but she's pregnant with her fifth. Belly like a barrage balloon and those corsets pinch something fierce when you've got a bit of padding to contend with. Besides, you don't want all that exercise when you're about to drop do you?'

Bracewell had a sudden coughing fit and Cooper shot her a venomous look. To Alice he said: 'Just tell us about Miss Dunphy.'

'Who? Oh, Brenda you mean? Funny, I never knew her last name. Poor cow. I just used to call her Pussy.' Alice's eyes began to redden. She retrieved a handkerchief from her bra strap and blew her nose loudly.

'Why did you call her Pussy when her name was Brenda?' Cooper wanted to know, completely missing the warning signs Patty was frantically trying to semaphore in his directions with her eyes.

'It's her porn name,' Alice told him. 'Pussy Queen. You know how to work out your porn name don't you, Inspector?'

As Cooper struggled for an answer, Alice expanded his knowledge of world events.

'You take the name of your first pet and the street where you lived as a kid and put them together. Pussy, sorry, Brenda, used to live on Queen Street when she was little. She told me she adopted a mangy stray cay she found in the garden. Thought the world of it. She called it Pussy. Not very imaginative but she was only four. Anyway, that's how she came up with the name. Pussy Queen. She thought it was funny, considering.'

'Yes, well,' Cooper managed, ignoring the grin on Patty's face. This is why I never asked for a transfer to vice, he told himself. Something about women like Dirty Alice unnerved him. Winkle had always been good at this sort of thing but it made Cooper feel like a schoolboy. 'You were saying?' he prompted.

'Well, I knew she was hard up. Always going on about it in the pub and she wasn't bad looking. Had good biceps. Always a good sign in my line of work that.'

Bracewell made a wheezing sound that turned rapidly into hiccups. 'Do you want to leave the room, DC Bracewell?' Cooper asked.

Bracewell shook her head. 'No Sir,' she squeaked. 'Sorry Sir.'

'So I should think. Go on Mrs Palmer.'

'Miss. I never took his name.' She smiled coquettishly. Cooper waved encouragement.

'Miss Palmer,' he said. 'Go on, please.'

'Well, she wasn't keen at first. Said she didn't think she'd have the time. I told her it would only be for a couple of weeks and she could keep whatever she made and she finally said she'd do it. I told her she wouldn't have to touch them or anything.' Alice made a hand gesture. 'Maybe the odd handshake, but that's it, I swear.' Bracewell made a hissing noise like a gasket about to explode. 'I showed her where I keep the bucket and mop and everything,' Alice continued. Bracewell exploded from her chair and made for the door, her hand over her mouth. As it slammed shut behind her, Cooper could hear her bellow with laughter in the corridor.

'Is she all right?' Alice wanted to know.

'Convent school,' Cooper told her. Alice nodded.

'Thought so,' she said. 'I can always tell. If she ever wants to moonlight, give her my number. She'd be perfect for this game.'

Cooper sighed. He'd been right. It was going to be a

bloody long day. Silence descended as Cooper attempted to marshal his thoughts. Finally he said: 'You know that porn name thing you were talking about? The name of your first pet and the street where you lived as a kid wasn't it?' Alice nodded. Cooper sighed. 'On that basis I'd be Tiny Littlewick,' he said.

'You wouldn't get much work,' Alice said.

30

Her name was Swan now.

Swan was such an exotic name, she told herself.

Much better than her given name.

Christopher.

And so appropriate too, since she had now emerged from the ugly duckling Christopher to become a beautiful Swan.

The Paddock Bar was crowded. It always was. Gender amorphous patrons mixed and mingled with impunity. Vivienne, a hefty tranny in a bottle green dress, dangly earrings and three day stubble, said: 'Fresh meat at the bar. He's new, but he's been blanking everyone who's made a move so far.'

'He just hasn't met the right girl, that's all,' Swan giggled.

Vivienne sniffed. 'He's a tourist if you ask me. Just seeing the sights but not interested in becoming part of the attraction. Even Samantha tried and got knocked back.'

'Samantha? That slapper. He was just showing good taste, that's all.'

Vivienne shrugged. 'I don't know. There's something off about him.'

'Nonsense. He just needs a bit of encouragement. Watch this.'

With that, Swan smoothed down her dress and made her way through the crowded bar. He was sitting by himself at the counter. Most of the patrons were men, a good half of which were wearing women's clothes with varying degrees of success. The newcomer was wearing slacks and a check shirt, a light jacket slung over the back of his bar stool. He had blonde hair and a slim build. She couldn't tell the colour of his eyes, but she was certain they had to be blue.

The seats on either side of him were taken, but that was soon solved. A short, dark haired boy in a black tee-shirt and jeans, wearing too much mascara was on his left. Swan walked up to him and tapped him on the shoulder. He turned to look at her.

'Does your mother know you're here?' she said. The youth paled. Swan jerked her head towards the door. The youth scrambled down from his stool and left in a hurry. Swan smiled. She could always tell the underage ones. It had only been a couple of years since she was one of them, but she had more style and had never been asked to leave. She slid onto the vacated stool. Her target was staring straight ahead, apparently unaware of the altercation that had just taken place. Swan held out a slim, immaculately manicured hand with inch long red nails.

'Hi,' she husked. 'I'm Swan.'

He turned to look at her. Blue eyes she noticed. He stared at her for several seconds, then took her hand gently in his. 'I'm ...' he began but Swan placed an elegant red tipped finger across his lips to silence him.

'You are adorable, that's what you are,' she said, and ran a long nail down his cheek. 'Buy me a drink darling and I'll tell you my life story.'

'I'm waiting for someone,' he said.

'And I'm right here, darling. Your waiting is over.'

He shook his head. 'I mean someone special. I'm waiting for Nancy.'

Swan's lipsticked mouth made an "O". 'So, you're a "special". Is that why you've been knocking back all those others?'

'Yes. Besides which, they weren't as pretty as you.'

'Flattery will get you everywhere.'

'Is there somewhere we can go? Somewhere private.'

'I only live ten minutes away. How does that sound?'

'Perfect.'

Vibienne watched them go. 'That bitch has all the luck,' she muttered and turned her attention to an inebriated brickie from Wolverhampton who had only wandered in to use the loo but would soon have a life-changing experience.

*

Swan put the kettle on to boil and spooned coffee into the cups. 'How do you take your coffee?' she asked.

'As it comes.' His voice was closer than she anticipated and she turned to find him standing in the kitchen doorway stark naked.

She smiled. 'That's a bit forward of you,' she said. 'I thought this was purely a blood thing.'

He shrugged. 'No harm in having a little fun as well is there?'

'None whatsoever.' Swan moved forward, her hand reaching between his legs and something hard punched her just below the ribs. She grunted, her mouth open in shock. She felt her knees buckle as she slid down his body to the floor.

'Sorry to disappoint,' he said. 'I just didn't want to get my clothes all bloody.'

And then he began to cut.

A neighbour noticed Swan's front door open the next morning and discovered the mutilated corpse. They did what any concerned citizen would do. They phoned the local and national newspapers and negotiated a fee before calling the police. DCI Cooper didn't have a chance of keeping this out of the public domain. The press would be calling for someone's head on a platter and he had a pretty good idea whose head that would be.

31

'Nicotine and caffeine. That's what you need.'

Trixie filled the kettle and placed it on the stove. Dolly took a packet of cigarettes from her pocket, lit one and placed it between Tink's unresponsive lips. Outside the tiny staff kitchen, the usual afternoon noises of Denby Lodge continued unabated. On the TV someone was buying and selling tat masquerading as antiques; the steady tap, tap, tap of walking frames traversing the corridor; the occasional hum of a motorised wheelchair; the muted buzz of voices punctuated now and then by a raucous laugh as Mr Baxter told the ladies one of his off-colour jokes – again. Trixie set out three cups, spooned coffee into each of them, came and sat at the table. Tink sat immobile, cigarette drooping at a 45% angle. Trixie looked across at Dolly. 'Is he all right?' she asked. 'He's very quiet.'

'Shock,' Dolly said. 'And his aura's a very funny colour.'

At that moment, Tink let out a low, bovine moan, his shoulders began to shake and his face crumpled like a day old newspaper. Large tears began to course down his cheeks and the cigarette wobbled dangerously on his lower lip. Dolly patted his hand. 'There, there, that's better. Let it all out. Your aura's looking better already.'

'Your face isn't,' Trixie told him. 'Your mascara's running.'

Dolly shushed her, but Tink gave a large sniff and wiped the heel of his hand across his eyes.

'Never use mascara,' he said. 'This is all natural.'

Trixie patted his other hand. 'That's my boy,' she said. Tink took the cigarette from his mouth and looked at it like it was an alien life-form. 'What the hell am I doing sucking on this?'

he said.

'Bet that's not the first time you've said that,' Trixie murmured.

'I've been off the fags for ages,' Tink moaned, ignoring her. 'Six months of vaping gone west that is.'

Dolly reached out to take the cigarette from him. 'I'll take it away,' she said.

'May as well finish it now I've started,' Tink said, and took a long drag. He exhaled a long plume of smoke along with a question: 'Why Swan?'

'She was just in the wrong place at the wrong time, that's all,' Trixie said.

'Is that all it was?'

'What else could it be?'

Tink pouted and stubbed the cigarette out in a convenient saucer. 'She wasn't like the others,' he said. 'She wasn't on the game, she was just ... lovely. Poor, lovely, delicate Swan.' Tink's lip began to quiver. 'And who's next, that's what I want to know. It could be any one of us.'

The kettle began its shrill whistle as they stared forlornly at each other.

32

Better to ask forgiveness than permission, isn't that what they say? A priest would know all about forgiveness, but what if his own acts were unforgiveable? And he certainly never asked permission. Oh, Mother may have acquiesced, bartered her flesh for the saving of her son's soul but the priest still took advantage of two damaged people for his own evil ends.

'Forgive me.'

He keeps saying it over and over again.

'Forgive me.' 'Forgive me.' 'Forgive me.' 'Forgive me.' 'Forgive me.' 'Forgive me.'

He thinks it might help. Thinks it might save him. He's wrong. So very, very wrong.

When it was over, the voice asked:

Did you enjoy that?

'Oh, yes. Very much.

There will be more. Just for you. But now we have my work to complete, yes?

'Yes,' That only seemed fair. The others could wait. He knew who would be next on his list. The thought made him smile.

33

His hands were tied together in an attitude of prayer. Blood in the nave and all along the pews suggested that his road to the altar had been a long and arduous one. His clothes were found in a bag of donations for the poor and needy. Cooper looked at the ribbons of flesh that hung from ecclesiastical bones and tried to block out the clamour coming from outside the church. No way could they keep the lid on this. The cleaner who had discovered the good father had alerted the press before dialling 999 no doubt. And then the gossip mill began to churn. Soon, an army of outraged parishioners, press, newspapers and gawkers were camped out on the doorstep. Cooper could imaging the Bishop dialling the Chief Constable's number right this second. He needed a result and he needed it fast.

'Might as well pray for it,' he muttered. 'I'm in the right place'

34

Winkle had to get away from Ida's kindly but suffocating scrutiny. Kicking against the traces was fine within the confines of the force, but when you were on your own you realised the traces were the only thing keeping you upright. Grief, and his inability to function in the only role that had ever given his life meaning, led to depression which led to drink. A vicious circle. Ida became a mother hen and a jailer. He needed space. Needed air. Needed time to think.

His meeting with Sir Francis continued to rattle around in his head. Did he believe the old boy was really a blood sucking vampire? Of course not. Did he believe that Sir Francis and Dolly and God knows who else were some sort of sex fetishists whose numbers may include someone deranged enough to commit multiple murders to satisfy their fantasy? You bet.

'A speedy and discrete solution to this problem would benefit all concerned, don't you agree?' That's what Sir Francis had said to him. As Dolly had led him out she had said:

'I know it's a lot to take in, but please consider Sir Francis's offer. And you won't have to do it alone?'

'Won't I?'

'No. I can help. I'd like to. Every Sherlock Holmes needs his Doctor Watson. Every Lone Ranger his Tonto. Every Batman his Robin.'

'Every Eric his Little Ern?'

'Now you're teasing. But I mean it. I have access to resources that you may not. I'll keep in touch.'

Threat or promise, Winkle wasn't sure, but as leads go it

may be thin but it was all he had. For now at least. After promising Ida that he would call her if he needed anything, or even just felt like a chat, Ida had reluctantly left for work. Winkle had followed soon after with the vague notion of a lunchtime drink. Once outside, the notion had receded somewhat. He just felt empty. Hollow as a drum. He let his feet take him where they would. He idly browsed the shop windows that ringed the market place. Sometimes it would take him by surprise. A magazine in a newsagents that Peggy had always liked. A dress in a shop window that looked like one that Peggy used to wear. Sometimes just his own reflection in a shop window that reminded him that that sad, lonely figure was all that he had left now. And the tears would start to flow.

'Are you all right, love?' Maggie, from the Old Slappers Coffee Club, all fur coat and probably no knickers, encroached upon his personal space with cheap scent and genuine emotion. A tart she was, but her heart beat with compassion whereas some days Winkle wasn't sure his was beating at all.

'Just got something in my eye,' he said.

Maggie raised a carefully drawn eyebrow. 'Crying ain't nothing to be ashamed of. Nothing unmanly about it. I've got this one punter, big bloke, works the oil rigs, one look at my stocking tops and he's blubbing like a baby. Doesn't stop until I pull the trigger on his fun gun, if you know what I mean.'

'I do. And I wish I didn't.'

Maggie stared at him for a second, then she shrugged her shoulders and carried on.

'I've got something that'll cheer you up.'

'Oh, yea?' said Winkle dubiously, hoping it had nothing to

do with the aforementioned stocking tops.

'You said to get in touch if we heard anything.'

'Have you?'

'Not me. Suzy. She's just come back from her holidays. Swears blind she knows who this bastard is.'

'Take me to her.'

*

The Grapes was a back street pub that even Winkle had not frequented. Small, run down and covered in a layer of grime. Suzy looked about the same. A skinny, dyed blonde with a creosote tan. She was knocking back a vat sized glass of wine like they were about to re-introduce prohibition and she wanted to stock up. Winkle raised an eyebrow in Maggie's direction.

'All right,' Maggie admitted, 'so she has a bit of a drink problem, but I swear she's telling the truth about this bloke. When she heard about the murders, how they were done, she went pale as milk, and that takes some doing with Suzy.'

'I believe you,' muttered Winkle. 'All right, let's see what she knows.'

Maggie made the introductions and they sat down.

'Tell him what you told me,' Maggie urged.

'Well,' Suzy said, 'this is going back a few years, mind. More than twenty in fact, but when I heard about what had been done to those girls, it made my blood run cold. It must be the same bloke. There can't be two like him surely.'

'What bloke is this?' Winkle urged.

'This punter, not bad looking, but a real mean sort. Liked it rough. More than rough. He used to pay the girls extra to let him cut them. He liked to see them bleed the dirty bugger, and then...' She paused and her eyes took on a far-away look.

'Go on,' said Winkle. 'What did he do then?'

'He used to lick up all the blood, just like a bleedin' vampire. The more the better.'

'You're sure about all this?' Winkle asked.

'I'm sure all right. I was one of his regulars. He left me with a few souvenirs.' Suzy reached down and pulled her sweater up under her chin exposing her belly and walnut sized breasts. A ragged cheer went up from the bar. Winkle ignored them, staring instead at the criss-cross pattern of thin scars that laced her flesh, visible as pale lines even through her tan. He motioned with his hand and Suzy lowered her sweater.

'He liked to cut deep, the bastard. Wasn't as if I could go to the hospital or anything. They never really healed. Now I just tell people I got them from a fight with a jealous wife.' She gave a throaty chuckle. 'Got the idea from a madam who used to work this manor. Pretty girl she was, but she had a scar that ran right across her cheek. She told punters that she got it from an Arab sheik. The Hooray Henry's lapped it up, daft sods.'

A shadow fell across them. The landlord pointed a stubby finger at Suzy.

'Oy! This is a respectable pub,' he said with as straight a face as he could muster. 'If you want to show the punters the merchandise, rent a bloody shop window.'

'Police business,' Winkle growled. 'So bugger off and leave us alone.'

The landlord sniffed. 'You got any ID?' he said.

'You got a licence for that slot machine?' Winkle replied.

The landlord considered his options for a second or two, then contented himself with a sniff in their direction as he headed back behind the bar. Winkle turned back to Suzy.

'This punter,' he said, 'did he have a name?'

'Might have. It was so long ago, I don't know if I can remember it now.'

Winkle sighed and reached into his jacket for his wallet. Maggie put a restraining hand on his arm. 'You're not paying her for this,' she said. 'She's gonna do this for free.'

Suzy pouted. 'Girl's got to live,' she said.

Maggie leaned forward. 'This is Peggy's fella,' she whispered.

Suzy paled beneath the mahogany finish. 'Strewth! I never knew, honest, otherwise I'd never have tried it on. She was a good girl was Peggy.'

Winkle felt walls begin to crumble in his heart. 'The name,' he said gruffly, 'what was his name?'

'Blood,' she said. 'Barry Blood.'

35

'Barry Blood!' Winkle fumed. 'Barry sodding Blood!' They were walking by the canal, arm in arm, just like a normal couple going for a romantic stroll beside a rat infested open sewer. There must be a metaphor in there somewhere Winkle thought but was too tired to think what it might be.

'Sorry, Winkle,' Ida said. 'Maggie thought she was being helpful. Still, do you think she was telling the truth?'

Winkle grunted. 'She probably was, the addled cow. Too rat-arsed to know that Barry Blood's been dead these twenty years.'

Barry Blood had been a local celebrity. A horror rocker with three hit singles and a hit album behind him before he wrapped his car around a tree, a victim of too much fame, whiskey and heroin.

Winkle scratched his head. 'Still,' he said, 'those scars looked similar. Maybe Barry wasn't the only one into the vampire schtick. It might be worth looking into. There's bugger all else to go on from what I hear.'

'You'll find him Winkle,' Ida said. 'I have faith in you.'

'Just like the Mountie's me. I always get my man.'

'And when you find him,' she said, 'you'll turn him over to the proper authorities, yea?'

Winkle nodded. 'Eventually,' he said. 'Eventually.'

Dolly phoned later that evening. Winkle told her about Barry Blood.

'Before my time,' Dolly said. 'I'll ask Sir Francis. If he was an active member of the brotherhood, Sir Francis will know.'

'If he doesn't,' Winkle told her, 'I know a man who might.'

36

Lenny Pepper pointed to a ginger wig perched on a polystyrene head. 'That's Barnet,' he said, and ran his hand over his shiny scalp. 'I only wear him for public appearances and publicity shots. It's a better image.' He picked up a pile of vinyl albums and began shuffling them like an oversized deck of cards. 'Lost all my hair when I was fourteen. Just happened overnight, nobody knows why. Ever since I've not had a single hair anywhere on my body. I'll show you if you want.'

Winkle shook his head. 'I'll take your word for it.'

'There's a name for it, but I can never remember it.'

'Alopecia.'

'Bless you!' Lenny grinned. 'Just my little joke.'

'Very little.'

'So, what can I do for you, Inspector? Personal appearance at the policeman's ball, is it? If it's about those parking tickets, the cheque is in the post.'

'Nothing like that. And it's Sergeant.'

'There's still time.'

'Does the name Suzy Broadbent mean anything to you?'

Lenny frowned in concentration. 'Can't say it does. Should it?'

'She knows you.'

'The price of fame, Inspector. Sorry, Sergeant.'

'It was some time ago. Twenty years or so.'

'Oh, well. I can't remember what I had for breakfast, or even if I had breakfast, so twenty years ...'

'I'll jog your memory. The last time you saw her she would have been naked. And covered in blood.'

Lenny fumbled the stack of albums and they cascaded onto the floor, some falling out of their covers in the process. The reception of Full Moon FM had the most awful piece of carpeting Winkle had ever seen. A green and brown combat motif that built up so much static electricity it was a miracle Barnet wasn't standing on end like a Halloween fright wig. The only other room in the garden shed complex was the broadcast studio. Full Moon FM was a local commercial station, permanently on its uppers, with Lenny Pepper as its owner and main, sometimes only, broadcaster. Lenny levered himself onto his knees and began gathering up his vinyl chicks into his protective embrace.

'Oh,' he said, avoiding Winkle's eyes. 'That Suzy Broadbent. Do someone a favour and its bound to come back and bite you in the arse,' he grumbled.

'You call slicing her up like a salami doing her a favour?'

'I had nothing to do with that!' Lenny said sharply. 'That was all Baz. Barry Blood that is.' Lenny held out his hand and Winkle hauled him to his feet. They sat on rickety kitchen chairs at a small table. 'What do you want to know?' Lenny asked resignedly.

'You were Barry Blood's manager. What was he like?'

'Talented little fucker. But weird as they come.'

'Go on.'

'His band, the Blood Clots, were about to make it big. Goth, punk rock, horror shockers. They had it all. But Barry ...' Lenny shook his head, the fluorescent light casting reflections from his sweaty dome. 'Barry took it all much too seriously.'

'And the others didn't?'

'No. They were talented musicians, but it was just a pose

for them. Pills and pussy. That's all they were in it for. And there was plenty of that, I can tell you.'

'Which brings us to Suzy Broadbent.'

'I didn't know her name. Dunno where Barry found her either. You have to understand, Barry really lived the role. He was like a method actor. In real life he was just Bob Hutton, failed electrician, but on stage he was Barry Blood, vampire lord out to ravish virgins and drink their blood. He really believed it, the daft sod.'

'Is that what he did to Suzy?'

Lenny snorted. 'She wasn't a virgin, I can tell you that much. Just some slapper he picked up I suppose. We used to rehearse in a hall on Osborne Road. We all turned up one day and found them. She was stretched out on the floor. Naked. Tied and gagged. And Barry ...' Lenny shuddered.

'Go on,' Winkle urged.

'He was cutting her. Blood everywhere. It took hours to get the stains out of the floor. We couldn't have left them there or the scouts would have had a nightmare.'

'Never mind the scouts. What about Barry Blood.'

'Like I say, he was cutting her. It was horrible. Even the Clots were shocked. We just piled in and pulled him off her. I untied her.' He paused, then: 'Long story short, I gave her a wad of cash to keep her mouth shut. That sort of publicity would have ruined the band's chances. I mean, they like a bit of stage gore, but this was way out of line. He could have gone to prison and that would really have fucked us up. We didn't know it then, but we were fucked anyway. Dozy bugger. Anyway, she seemed happy enough with the arrangement at the time, so she's got no reason to start complaining now.'

'She's not. What happened to Barry after that?'

'Well, everyone was on edge. The album had just come out and we had some gigs lined up. If he went psycho on stage it would have been a disaster.'

'So what happened next?'

'The lads took him out for a drink.'

Lenny stopped. Winkle waited and then prompted: 'That was the night he died.'

'Yea. He got drunk. Took a few snorts of talcum, insisted he was okay to drive and wrapped his car around a tree. Silver lining, album sales rocketed. Probably the best solution all round really. Not for Barry of course, but the rest of us did all right. I made enough to start this place.'

Winkle looked around at the shabby surroundings and figured there must either be a lot of overheads in setting up your own radio station or album sales were nowhere near as rocket-like as Lenny pretended they were, but said: 'How fortunate.'

'That's rock 'n' roll for you.'

'Where are the rest of the band now?'

'We don't keep in touch. Sid went to America, became some sort of street artist. Ron makes porn movies and Chas ... dunno. He was only the drummer.'

Winkle heaved himself to his feet. 'You've been very helpful, Lenny. If I need to speak to you again, I'll be in touch.'

'You know where to find me. Why so interested anyway?'

'Haven't you heard, Lenny? Vampires have a nasty habit of coming back from the dead.'

37

'And that's one of me and Barry at the Anvil Club. He'd just come off stage and he was all sweaty.'

Dolly looked at the middle-aged woman sitting on her sofa and tried to match her up with the doe-eyed girl in the blurry snapshot who seemed to think sweat was an aphrodisiac. She couldn't do it, but then, everyone does things when they're young that they regret later. Except Diane Metcalfe didn't seem to regret a thing. That's why she was still President of the Clotettes, the official Barry Blood and the Blood Clots fan club and the only other person Dolly could think of who might know anything at all about Barry Blood's more eccentric proclivities. When Sir Francis had been able to offer no insight into who Barry Blood might have been, Dolly had decided to turn detective. A quick internet search had turned up trumps. The Clotettes still had a Facebook page and an even more convenient phone number.

'There's only three of us now,' Diane had told her when Dolly had phoned her. 'All the others lost interest, but not me, Avril and Maureen. Clotette's till we die, that's us.'

Dolly had refrained from telling her that may be sooner than you think and asked her if she would answer a few questions about Barry and the boys. It turned out that Diane would be delighted to talk about the heady days of Bloodmania. Stopping her was the problem. She even brought a box of souvenirs; posters, programmes, newspaper articles, a tatty piece of cloth that was, supposedly, one of Barry's scarves. 'Never been washed,' Diane said, proudly. 'But you can touch it if you want.'

With deference to the comment about sweat, Dolly politely declined the invitation and Diane placed it back in its plastic bag. 'Of course, we followed them round all over', Diane said. 'Sometimes we'd cadge a lift in their van. Sometimes we hitchhiked. Couldn't do that now of course, far too risky.'

Slightly less risky than getting chummy with a psycho whose idea of fun was to carve his initials into your naked flesh, Dolly thought, but said nothing.

'Everyone had their favourite in the band. We even had their names tattooed on our arms. My Mum went mental. Look.' She rolled up her sleeve and showed some faded, blotchy calligraphy on the inside of her right forearm.

Barry
Sid
Ron

'I thought there were four of them?' Dolly said.

'There was. The other one was only the drummer.' She rolled her sleeve back down. 'But for me, it was Barry or nothing. We knew he was married of course, but that didn't stop us waiting outside his house, hoping to catch a glimpse of him. Daft I suppose but we were young.'

'Married?' Dolly interrupted.

'Yea. Had a kiddie as well. A boy I think. Yea, definitely a boy. Robbie his name was. Called him after his dad. That was Barry's real name you see. Bob.' She smiled, pleased that she knew this particular piece of rock trivia.

'And you knew where he lived? You waited outside his house?'

'Yes. It was nothing special. You wouldn't think a rock god lived there.'

Dolly ignored the deification of a sweaty sadist and said:

'Where did he live? Exactly.'

'Twenty-seven Burnham Road. Nice road it was. Very neat.'

Dolly was no longer listening. She was on her feet, ushering Diane out of the door, thanking her very much for a most interesting chat but she had an urgent call she had to make. As soon as the front door was closed on a flustered Diane, Dolly grabbed her phone and dialled Winkle's number.

38

'One more.' He bit his lip to stop himself saying "please". The voice was getting harder to resist, but he knew that as long as the voice needed him to carry out the physical acts of vengeance he held the upper hand. He had no idea who these women were or why the voice wanted them dead. It was some insane master plan that made sense only to the voice, but as long as he got his way he was prepared to go along with it. As long as he got his turn. It was only fair after all.
Very well
He smiled and dialled the number.

39

The phone rang just as Trixie was about to get to level 5 of Smash and Grab 3. She swore and picked up her phone. She didn't recognise the number.

'Hello?' she said.

There was a pause and then a quiet voice said: 'It's me.'

'Who's me?'

'Robbie.'

She almost hung up. Would have done, should have done, but he sounded so pathetic. He always had been, really. At best, it had been a sympathy shag to give him something to remember when his sour-faced old mother was nagging him. At worst, it was her own inner demon daring her to see if someone so downtrodden could actually get it up.

'What do you want?' she said.

A pause. Then: 'A haircut.'

Trixie laughed out loud. 'A haircut! And I suppose that psycho bitch of a mother of yours is going to kick me out into the street stark bollock naked again is she? I nearly got arrested last time, standing there with my tits and arse on show, do you know that?'

'I didn't know. I'm sorry. It won't happen again. Mother is …'

'What? On medication? Locked up in a loony bin where she belongs?'

'Dead.'

'Oh!' It took the wind out of her sails. 'I'm sorry,' she muttered. 'I didn't know.'

'Maybe this was a bad idea.'

'No. No. It's all right. A haircut? Yea?' Christ, she was

feeling sorry for him now.
'Yes, a haircut. Please.'
'Okay. What time?'

40

Trixie's arms hurt. So did her throat, but her arms ached like they were being pulled out of their sockets. She jerked herself awake, memory flooding in. The bastard! He tried to strangle me! She raised her head with an effort. No wonder her arms hurt. Her hands were tied at the wrist and suspended through a pulley fixed to the ceiling. When she was unconscious, she had slumped forward, putting all her weight on her arms and shoulders. She managed to plant her feet on the floor and stand up. It eased the pain in her shoulders, but she was still shackled. And naked. She could see her clothes piled on a chair. The kinky bastard. She tried to assess what else he might have done to her whilst she was unconscious. Apart from the pain in her arms and shoulders, she didn't feel any different. Slowly she took in her surroundings. Posters, amplifiers, musical instruments.

'Where the fuck am I?' she muttered, and pain sliced through her buttocks, a single, piercing, all enveloping pain.

She screamed: 'Jesus fuck!' and sweat broke out on her skin. There was a movement behind her and a figure came into view. Robbie. Dressed in black leather trousers and a red silk shirt. He held a long, sharp, knife in his hand. The blade was tinged with red. Blood. Her blood.

Trixie shook sweat from her eyes. 'What the fuck have you come as?' she muttered.

Attitude didn't seem to faze him. 'They belonged to my father,' he said. 'This was his room. It seemed appropriate.' He gestured to the ropes that held her. 'Sorry if you're uncomfortable,' he said. 'I could have done this with you sitting down, but I wanted access to every inch of you. I got the idea from that stupid dominatrix. I had to improvise, but I think I did a pretty good job, don't you agree?'

Cold fear swamped Trixie's system. She thought for a minute she was going to pass out but fought it off. 'You won't get away with this,' she said. Sounded lame even to her own ears.

'Oh, but I already have. Many times.'

'They know where I am.' Desperate.

'I doubt that. But even if it were true, they would be too late. Far, far too late.'

He came towards her and she saw he held a roll of tape in his hand. He tore off a strip and stuck it across her mouth. 'Don't want to disturb the neighbours, do we?'

He tossed the tape to one side and ran the edge of the knife slowly across her stomach and up to her breast, gently, almost caressingly, not hard enough to draw blood. Not yet.

'Now, 'he smiled. 'Where shall we start?'

41

Dolly met him at the corner. She was flushed, a mixture of excitement, anticipation and fear. It was a quiet, residential street. Neat gardens, fresh paint on glass panelled front doors. The sort of neighbourhood where you expected net curtains to twitch at the sight of strangers. Definitely not the sort of place you expected to find a serial killer.

Also not the place you expected to see a pink motorbike and sidecar combination, but there one was, parked incongruously outside number twenty-seven. The sight of it stopped Winkle in his tracks. He fished out his mobile phone and dialled Trixie's number. He let it ring a dozen times, then hung up and dialled again. Ida picked up.

'Where are you?' she said.

'Outside twenty-seven Burnham Road. Write that number down. If I don't ring back in an hour, call Tommy and tell him to get here pdq.'

'What's going on Wink?'

'I think I've got him.'

'And you plan to do what? You're not bloody Rambo. Don't do anything until I get there.'

'Can't wait that long. I think Trixie's inside'

'What? Wink, you have to call Cooper.'

'No time. You call him in an hour. Not before. This bastard is mine. Don't worry. I've got back-up.'

And he hung up.

42

The front door was locked. No sound came from inside. Winkle led Dolly to the back of the house. An untended garden welcomed them. That and a conveniently unlocked patio door. The place was so ordinary it screamed abnormality. Moving quickly but quietly, Winkle checked out the downstairs rooms. Nothing. He paused at the bottom of the stairs. A faint sound filtered down to them. He pressed a finger to his lips. In a whisper he said: 'Wait here.' Dolly tried to protest, but Winkle hushed her. 'Wait,' he repeated and began a heavy, careful tread upwards.

A Fender Stratocaster is a fine instrument. Solid bodied and well built. A real piece of craftsmanship. Winkle had always wanted to see one close up. As he crossed the upstairs landing and pushed tentatively at the partly opened bedroom door, he was forcefully reminded of the saying: "be careful what you wish for."

Wielded with considerable force, that was what hit Winkle full in the ribs, breaking two and knocking him back onto the landing. He hadn't seen his assailant. Hadn't been looking. He'd been transfixed by Trixie. Trixie dressed in red from head to toe. But not dressed at all. Winkle instinctively moved towards her. As he did so he felt the whistle of air as the Fender crashed into him, sending him flying.

Winkle heaved himself upright, pain like fire screaming through him, and threw himself headlong into the room. This time he saw the Fender coming. Winkle grabbed it and hung on, swinging the mad axe-man around in a circle, trying to get him off balance. Their momentum knocked them into Trixie making her swing like a punchbag hit with a roundhouse right, then she stuck out her foot between the killer's legs. He stumbled. Winkle held on to the Fender as he fell, wrenching it from his grasp. The force of the manoeuvre threw Winkle off balance. He stumbled against the wall, came forward to meet another charge as his attacker came up from his knees. He punched Winkle hard, in the stomach. Winkle had been punched before, but it hadn't hurt like this. He looked down into a grinning face and saw the hilt of a knife sticking out of his own stomach. Confident now, Robbie Hutton, if that's who this was, and, Winkle reasoned, who else could it be, rose to his feet, still holding the knife, twisting, ripping, the handle now slick with Winkle's blood. Winkle had a brief glimpse of Trixie's eyes widen with fear and then his senses were swept away on a wave of pain and nausea. He slumped to his knees and felt the blade withdraw. He put up an arm and felt the blade descend, slicing through to the bone. Not now, he thought. Not now when I'm so close. Winkle commanded his legs to work, to get him onto his feet, but they refused to respond. He saw the black and red horror tower above him, knife poised. Then Robbie's head jerked back and he screamed. He staggered forward. There, behind him, a bloody scalpel in her hands, stood Dolly Boone. She sliced him with the pick sticker she used on herself in the alley! 'You go, girl,' Winkle whispered. Or at least, he thought he whispered it, he couldn't really tell. All he knew for sure was that Robbie was turning towards Dolly, knife drawn back, ready to lunge.

'No!' this time he did more than whisper. Winkle screamed the word, lunged forward, grabbed Robbie around the waist and heaved backwards with all his might. Both of them hit the window. Winkle felt it crack and splinter. There was one second of mad vertigo as they balanced precariously on the sill. And then they fell.

43

Winkle didn't feel the impact. Not as pain. He was beyond that. A jarring thud and then he was still. He sensed a broken body lying beneath him. Through fading eyes he saw the neck twisted at an obscene angle. Through bloodied lips, Winkle smiled and breathed a sigh. He heard the sound of footsteps. He knew they would be too late but he didn't care.

Dolly knelt beside him, tears cascading down her face. She grabbed his wrist and took his pulse. She took her phone from her pocket and made two calls. The second call was for an ambulance.

44

The first car to arrive on the scene was a blood red Lagonda V12. Sir Francis Varney levered himself out of the driver's seat and hurried around the side of the building to the scene of devastation.

The sight that greeted him brought him up short. Dolly was on her knees giving CPR to a bloody carcass that bore a strong resemblance to Winkle. To one side the twisted corpse of a young man who could only be the latest avatar of Ferenc Nadasdy. Varney gave him a cursory glance and dropped to arthritic knees beside Dolly.

'I got here as fast as I could,' he said. 'The old girl hasn't been out of the garage in thirty years but she performed admirably.'

Varney's mode of transport held little interest for Dolly Boone. 'Can-you-save-him?' she panted between compressions.

Varney reached out and stilled her hands. He placed his own hand on Winkle's chest, studied his blood-soaked face and shook his head. 'His injuries are too severe. The only option is to turn him.'

'Then do it,' Dolly told him. 'He doesn't deserve to die like this.'

'Is that what he would want?' Varney asked.

'I don't give a flying fuck what he wants!' Dolly shouted, for once in her life ignoring the polite protocols that had always governed her relationship with Sir Francis. 'It's what he deserves. It's what his friends want. He saved a young woman's life today. If he hadn't, God knows how many more would have died. Including you.'

Varney bowed his head. 'Your chastisement is justified and I apologise for my careless words, but what you ask is almost impossible. In my prime, maybe, but he would need more blood than I can possibly give. I just would not have the strength to effect the turning.'

Dolly rolled up her sleeve. 'Then take my strength,' she said. 'My blood revitalises you. Take it and give your blood to Winkle.'

Varney patted her hand. 'My dear, the effect will very likely drain both of us beyond our endurance.'

'You wan't blood, you can have mine.'

They both looked up, startled at the new voice. Trixie, naked and covered in blood walked unsteadily across the grass. Dolly stood up and rushed to her side.

'Trixie! I told you to rest. The ambulance will be here any time now.'

'Sod the ambulance,' Trixie said. As they passed Robbie's mangled corpse, Trixie lashed out with her bare foot and kicked him in the head. 'This fucker carved me up like a Christmas turkey. If Winkle hadn't saved me I'd be dead now, so if you need more blood for a transfusion or something, take mine.' So saying she slumped to her knees next to Winkle. From the street the sound of the second car to arrive on the scene could be heard screeching to a halt. A door slammed and they heard footsteps.

Varney reached out and held Trixie's hand. 'My dear, in your weakened state you are almost as much in need as Mr. Pilkington.'

'And it's not a normal transfusion,' Dolly said.

Another voice joined the chorus. 'Then stop buggering about and get on with it!' Ida Bone, red hair streaming behind her ran across the lawn and dropped to her knees.

'You've got three volunteers now. That's got to be enough, surely.'

'Well?' said Dolly. 'Will that be enough?'

Varney nodded. 'We shall try.' He nodded towards Trixie. 'But this young lady is in no fit state ...'

'I want to help,' Trixie insisited. 'He saved my life.'

'Stop farting about and get on with it!' Ida shouted.

'Very well,' Varney said, taking hold of Trixie's hand. 'This young lady first, but only a drop.' He bent his mouth to an open would that was still trickling blood.

'Don't you need a needle or anything?' Trixie asked.

'It's not that sort of transfusion,' Dolly told her again.

'Then what sort is ... whooooah!' Trixie's eyes flew wide open and her body spasmed. She began to make low moaning noises and her free hand roamed her breasts and between her legs frantically.

'Flamin' Nora, what's up with her?' Ida asked.

'I told you,' Dolly said. 'Best sex you've ever had.'

Trixie was jigging up and down, her hand clamped between her thighs as Varney removed his mouth from her arm. Producing a silver knife from his coat pocket, her opened a gash in his own arm and began feeding droplets of blood into Winkle's mouth. Trixie sank back onto her heels, running her tongue across her lips, her whole body flushed and shaking. 'That was so ... fucking ... amazing!' she said as she keeled over onto her side.

Dolly checked her pulse. 'Just fainted,' she said.

'All that just from one little bite?' Ida asked.

'Her weakened state didn't help, but, yes.'

'How many of those do you think Winkle's going to need?'

'Lots and lots,' Dolly said. 'And I don't think Trixie's in any fit state to donate any more, so it's up to you and me now.'

Varney raised his head. 'I need …' he began, but Ida didn't let him finish.

'I'm next,' she said. 'I'm next!'

*

When the ambulance arrived they found one definite corpse, one that might just as well have been, one aristocratic old gent looking decidedly shaky and three women, one naked and covered in blood, the other two fully clothed and pale as milk, but smiling. It would take a while for the police to piece together what had happened from the fractured stories of the surviving witnesses, but the conclusion was that Winkle had saved a young woman from being the latest victim of The Slasher and the papers played up his role of hero to the fullest extent. All the participants were taken to the hospital. Three were released later that day. One, Trixie, was kept in overnight for observation and one, identified as DS Roy "Winkle" Pilkington, was taken straight to Intensive Care, his chances slim to none in the opinion of all the medical staff.

45

Winkle's farewell was held at the Oxford Room at the Churchill Hotel. Up market and swanky, it was Winkle's idea of hell.

Cooper gave a speech, looking suitably uncomfortable.

'What can I tell you about Winkle,' he began. 'He was a pain in the arse.' Polite laughter. 'He was arrogant, rude, totally un-PC and the scruffiest bugger I've ever come across.' More laughter. 'He was also the best copper I've ever known and he'll be sorely missed.' That got a few "here, here's."

'True to form, he went out on a high note. Doing things his way, saving lives and catching a sadistic maniac in the process with no regard for his own safety.' That got even bigger cheers. 'To top it all, three days in a coma. And then he bounced back, if not quite as good as new, at least as bad tempered as ever.' Laughter. Cooper turned to the side of the stage where Winkle sat in his convalescent wheelchair, Ida standing behind him, Trixie, bandaged but smiling on one side and Dolly, resplendent in her best dress on the other next to Sir Francis.

'We're going to miss you, mate,' Cooper finished. Thunderous applause. Winkle ignored the many cries of "Speech, speech", telling them instead to lay waste to the bar.

Happy to do so, many came up to shake his hand and even crusty veterans had a hint of moisture in their eye.

'For Christ sake, get me to the buffet table,' Winkle growled. 'I've had enough sentiment to last me a lifetime. And I'm starving, so chop-chop.'

Ida dutifully complied and Winkle filled his plate with sandwiches, sausages on sticks, cheese, crisps and sausage rolls. He began to eat.

'So, Mr. Pilkington,' Varney said, 'what are your plans for your retirement?'

'Don't have any,' Winkle said. The letter from the hospital had arrived that morning. The appointment with the consultant was imminent and Winkle could not see a future beyond that diagnosis.

'He thinks he's going to die,' Ida said.

'That's right, tell the whole bloody world!' Winkle said.

Varney shook his head. 'I would not worry about that Mr. Pilkington,' he said. 'I predict a long, healthy future ahead of you.'

'A doctor now, are you?'

Varney simply smiled, but Dolly bent close. 'When a person is close to death and they imbibe of a vampire's blood they spend three days in a death like state until they are re-born as a true vampire,' she said.

'So what?' Winkle said around a mouthful of crumbs.

'So, you've just spent three days in a coma and ever since waking up you've been ravenously hungry. Maybe for something other than food?'

Winkle looked at her. 'Are you telling me you think I'm a bloody vampire?'

Ida shoved a sausage roll into his mouth. 'Not so loud,' she said. 'They've managed to keep their existence secret for hundreds of years. The last thing they want is you shouting the odds in a room full of nosy coppers.'

'Don't tell me they've bamboozled you with their bloody nonsense? I thought you had more sense. Load of old bollocks,' Winkle said.

'When you hit the ground, Winkle, you were dead,' Dolly told him. 'No way you could have survived. By the time I got there, I was sure you were heading for a slab. That's why I called Sir Francis.'

'It was touch and go,' Varney admitted. 'I barely made it there before the ambulance. And if it hadn't been for the help of these three ladies I fear that may have been the end of you even with my aid.'

'It's true Wink,' Ida said. 'We all chipped in.'

'Bit like a whip round,' Trixie said. 'Only the best flamin' whip round I've ever had,' she grinned.

'It was so Sir Francis was strong enough to feed you some of his blood.' Dolly said.

'He did what?'

'It's true, Wink,' Ida said. 'I don't know how else you could have survived. And if you hadn't been so bloody fat he wouldn't have needed to give you so much.'

'How else do you think you survived injuries like that?' Dolly asked.

'Good living and a hearty constitution.'

'Then how do you explain the hunger?' said Dolly.

'I'm a growing lad. And even if he did give me a blood smoothie, it wouldn't have made any difference. I've told you before, I don't believe in vampires.'

'Then it is your very good fortune, Mr. Pilkington,' Varney said softly, 'that we believe in you.'

Winkle paused, a sausage roll half way to his lips. He looked from one smiling face to the other. From Ida, to Dolly, to Trixie, to Varney. His stomach gurgled and the sausage roll lost its allure, replaced by a craving he had never known before, a craving for something ... other.

'Bloody hell,' he said. 'Bloody, bloody hell.'

Author's Note

Most of the characters and events in this book are real. I've just messed about with them to make them fit the story I wanted to tell because that's what writers do.

DEDICATION

This book is dedicated to my Grandad, the real William Walter John Colverson. He wasn't a policeman in Victorian London and he didn't fight vampires. He was just the best mate a boy could ever have.

Gary Orchard
August 2024

www.ingramcontent.com/pod-product-compliance
Lightning Source LLC
LaVergne TN
LVHW051827080426
835512LV00018B/2754